MIRACLES HAPPEN

ONE MOTHER

MIRACLES

ONE DAUGHTER

HAPPEN

ONE JOURNEY

Brooke and Jean Ellison

 HYPERION

NEW YORK

Miracles Happen is a memoir by Brooke and Jean Ellison. Conversations and situations are not all recounted exactly as they happened. They have been described to the best of our recollection and are not meant to be taken verbatim. While many of the names of the people in this book are accurate, some have been eliminated or changed to protect privacy.

Library of Congress Cataloging-in-Publication Data

Ellison, Brooke.
    Miracles happen : one mother, one daughter, one journey / Brooke and Jean Ellison.
        p. cm.
    ISBN 0-7868-6770-1
    1. Ellison, Brooke, 1978– 2. Quadriplegics—United States—Biography. I. Ellison, Jean, 1951– II. Title.

RC406.Q33 E45 2001
362.4'3'092—dc21
[B]
                                                                    2001024717

Book design by Casey Hampton

FIRST EDITION

10 9 8 7 6 5 4 3 2 1

Miracles Happen is dedicated to Edward Ellison. He saw us through every step of the process, and without his help, this book would not exist. His love, support, and encouragement have been a constant source of inspiration for us. He selflessly gives of himself in labors of love, teaching and sharing, guiding and caring. He is one of the biggest miracles in our lives. We love you.

ACKNOWLEDGMENTS

To Edward, Kysten, and Reed, for their unwavering devotion; our extended family, for the love they have given us; our friends, for being blessings in our lives; members of our community, for their support in our times of difficulty; teachers and professors, who have shared their knowledge; Harvard University, for their generosity; Jon Rosen and the William Morris Agency, for their help and guidance; Jennifer Lang and Hyperion Publishing, for their confidence in our ability; those who have touched our lives and changed them for the better.

THE CANDLE

Imprisoned in wax, I burn,
Slowly, steadily upward reaching.
I stretch, strain, ache to break free.
I remain immobile, kept to my appointed task,
Burn straight, burn bright.

My paraffin jailer keeps me focused,
Look not on the impenetrable layers,
That serve no other purpose.
See the light that emanates, illuminates,
Burn straight, burn bright.

What other meaning do I have?
Can some now see who were before in the dark?
I go unnoticed in the light of day,
But I am brightest when the room is dark.
Burn straight, burn bright.

I must burn now for my flame is fragile,
Easily snuffed by the breeze of a passerby.
Flickering, then, back on course—I stay alive.
The flame is who I am, not the wax.
Burn straight, burn bright.

—Brooke Ellison

PART ONE

A journey of a thousand miles begins with a single step.

—CONFUCIUS

PROLOGUE

THE RAYS OF LIGHT from the early morning sun were perfect as they streamed through my bedroom window. I've heard it said that these rays are the fingers of God that reach down to warm us and touch us. Dots of dust floated and swirled in and out of the light fleetingly and aimlessly. I couldn't help but think that they were like many of us, alone, believing life has no greater purpose. Are we just dots of dust, or is there something more? I used to be perplexed when my mother would throw her hands in the air, look to the ceiling, and say "What the hell is this all about?" after reading in the morning paper about some atrocity that man had perpetrated on himself. She would say to me, "Brooke, I only have one question that I want you to answer for me before I die: What is our purpose here?" I always felt that she was kidding, but the events of my life have taken me down a road where I have had to ask myself that question repeatedly. I think that I have come closer to an answer.

THE SUMMER OF 1990 had drawn to a close and as always the morning and evening air felt and smelled different. Nature, like the smell of a new pair of shoes or the feel of a new shirt, has its own way of letting everybody know that school is about to begin. It doesn't really matter how old you are, the impact is the same. It's almost Pavlovian. The smell of early-morning dew on the grass signals the stomach to churn, telling the brain to expect a steady diet of textbooks, ditto sheets, and homework assignments. I've always felt that the New Year really begins in September and that "Auld Lang Syne" should be sung on Labor Day, not on December 31. Our new year was about to begin and it seemed more full of promise than ever before. My mother, known to the rest of the world as Jean, was beginning a job, teaching some of the most difficult high school kids in a neighboring district. She had gone back to school three years earlier to get her teaching certificate and had just graduated in June. She wanted to help kids. September 4 was going to be *her* first day on the job and *my* first day starting the seventh grade at Murphy Junior High School.

My father, who works for Social Security, had taken the day off. He didn't want to miss either of our first days and felt the uncertainty that always goes along with new experiences. My mother seemed unusually apprehensive and distracted. It was not only her first day of work but also the first day of leaving us to fend for ourselves. My parents were a team, but with this new situation, more of the home responsibilities were beginning to shift to my father.

"Wardo?" I heard my mother call my father from the up-stairs hallway in one of those breathy whisper yells that people use when they want to be heard by only one person and no-body else. She always calls him Wardo, or honey, or sweetheart, depending on the nature of the conversation. I think that Wardo is a derivative of Eduardo, which is the Spanish or Ital-ian translation of his given name, Edward. It was early in the morning and my younger brother, Reed, and older sister, Kys-ten, were still sleeping.

"Wardo," she said again.

"Yes," he said from the kitchen table where both he and I were sitting.

"What time is Brooke's bus coming and where is it picking her up?" my mother asked. She has a way of asking questions to which she already knows the answer. It's her subtle way of making sure that everybody else knows, too.

My father walked to the refrigerator and grabbed a schedule that my mother had stuck there with one of those refrigerator magnets. Anything important got stuck on the refrigerator: doc-tor's appointment cards, telephone messages, interesting news-paper articles, and reminders from my mother on how we were supposed to live our lives.

"She gets picked up at nine and dropped off at one, at the

corner of Shetland and Sheppard," my father said as if it was something that he knew right off the top of his head.

My father and I looked at each other and smiled. We both understood that we were going to have to go through the itinerary of the day as many times as was necessary for my mother to feel secure that we knew exactly what we were supposed to do. My mother is a stickler for details and possibly the most organized and prepared person that I know. She can plan a meal two weeks in advance, and if she could have her way, she'd have the table set, too. We always had to know what we were doing, why we were doing it, and when it was going to be done—and be prepared for a pop quiz. She had just finished getting ready and had come down to sit with us for a few minutes before she had to leave.

"Your clothes are laid out on your bed," she said.

"Thanks, Mom."

"Don't forget your loose-leaf and new class schedule."

"I won't, Mom."

"Are you nervous?"

"A little bit, but don't worry, Ma, I'll be fine. How about you?" I said, trying to redirect her attention. She had enough to think about with her own new schedule without having to worry about mine.

"I'm fine, I just want to make sure that you guys know exactly what you're doing. It's hard for me to believe that you're starting the seventh grade, and look at you."

She stopped, put her hand on my shoulder and kissed me on my cheek.

"Don't forget to find out about orchestra and cello lessons," she continued as if never having lapsed from her mental checklist, "and dancing school starts this week so you'll have to work out how and when you're going to get your homework done."

"I know, Mom, I'll take care of it." There was a pause, one long enough to let us know that she had to go but really wanted to stay. She is an enigma, a beautiful enigma. She can be as tough as a marine drill instructor yet be reduced to tears over a simple act of kindness or a poignant song lyric. She got up from the table.

"Where's my clip? It's time for me to go," she said.

My mother is always losing her clip, the metal barrette she uses to hold up her long chestnut brown hair. She scanned the kitchen, checking all the likely hiding places—the sink top, the kitchen table, the counters—before spotting it on the strap of her pocketbook. She grabbed it and instinctively put it between her lips, twirled her hair, and completed the ritual by snapping the barrette into place. It was a maneuver I'd seen her do a thousand times.

"How do I look?" she said as she wrapped a lacy sash around her hips and tied it off just below her waist.

My mother's dark green pumps matched the light green floral print in her dress and accentuated her natural olive complexion. There were tears in her eyes that she was obviously fighting back.

"Wow, you look great, honey," my father said, shaking his head and smiling.

When he looked at her, I could tell that he knew how lucky he was. My mother and father met when they were sixteen years old. They were high school sweethearts. They were married at twenty-one and started the family at twenty-five. My brother and sister and I are all two years apart. My mother was even able to plan that, too.

"Brooke," my mother said, "I want you to remember everything that happens to you today so that when I come home we can talk about all of it. Don't forget anything, even the little things. Promise?"

I got the feeling that she was saying that not only because she was really interested, but also to try and compensate for some guilt she felt for leaving.

"I promise," I said, "and you do the same thing because I want to hear about your first day, too. Why don't you hurry up and get going and don't worry about us. You don't want to be late on your first day, do you?" I said. "Oh, Mom, don't forget that you have to pick out what you want for your birthday dinner tomorrow. Dad's cooking, so that means you have to figure out what kind of takeout you want!"

I was trying to get my mother off the hook. I could sense her dilemma, and as much as I wanted her to stay home, I also wanted her to go and know that everything would be all right. We were both starting out on new adventures, but neither one of us had any idea about the real journey on which we were both about to embark.

JEAN

I LEFT FOR WORK that morning in our 1978 green Chevy Nova, fondly known in our neighborhood as "the mean green machine." Ed and I hoped that with my new job we would be able to replace it. We didn't want anything extravagant, just a car with heat, air-conditioning, and a radio that worked. Ed and I were having trouble making ends meet. His job at Social Security was steady and dependable, but the paychecks barely covered the essentials. We were a family of five living on one salary on Long Island, where it takes at least two salaries just to turn the key to the front door of the house.

The seven-minute drive to work was a mental tug-of-war. I was beginning a new life and a new career, but I was also leaving my family. I was still a wife and a mother, this was most important, but now I was a teacher, too. I had to keep reminding myself that working was a necessity. I knew that I had to leave, but I also knew that I wanted to go. I felt that where I was going, I could possibly make a difference. My job wasn't going to be easy, I was going to be teaching kids that the mainstream had given up on. I wanted to have an impact on the lives of other children, as well as my own, especially the ones who didn't seem to get a fair shake in life. If I could do that, all of my hard work getting through college would have been worth it.

It was about 7:30 A.M. when I pulled into the parking lot at Unity Drive School. I checked myself in the rearview mirror. Like soot on a rain-soaked window, streaks of mascara and eyeliner had run down my cheeks. I had lost the battle to keep back my tears.

Although it was my first day on the job, the school and the staff were not unfamiliar to me. I had done my student teaching at Unity Drive and had made some good friends there. I had spent much of the summer preparing my new classroom, and Kysten, Brooke, and Reed had tagged along. I wanted my children to know what I was doing and for them to be a part of my new experience. They came armed with scissors, stencils, and staplers to help me out. Most of their time, however, was spent running in the empty halls and stairwells, looking for a soda machine that didn't exist.

I freshened my makeup, took a deep breath, and got out of the car. I was starting my new journey. I walked into the building and wondered how everything was at home.

BROOKE

IT WAS A SPECTACULAR DAY, the sun was radiant and warm but you could feel the crispness of fall in the air. My sister, Kysten, and brother, Reed, were scheduled to start school the next day, Reed the fifth grade and Kysten the ninth. The seventh-grade class was unique; we started school a day earlier than everyone else. September 4 was our orientation day, a day to be introduced to junior high. This would be our first time changing classes like the older kids. There were many nights when I stayed up flipping through the pages of my sister's junior high school yearbook, looking at all the pictures and reading all the names. It was hard for me to believe that I was finally going to be part of it all. I was so happy and so excited.

My father was outside on the deck finishing a cup of coffee. He had a peaceful and gentle expression on his face. His once red hair had since turned light brown and was beginning to grow thinner, a fact that bothered him more than he let on. His baggy sweatshirt and sweatpants didn't hide the fact that he was physically fit from years of marathon training. His appearance, especially with my mother on his arm, was always striking, yet he would never admit it.

I went out to sit with him after I was finished getting ready. I had painted my fingernails bright pink the night before, and had put three rhinestones on each of my ring fingers. My brightly colored fingertips were a contrast to the simple black and white outfit that I had picked out. Black patent leather oxfords with big floppy bows rounded out my first-day ensemble. My pink loose-leaf binder matched my nails by design and held about a dozen multicolored folders, one for each subject. My mother made sure that my class schedule was clearly visible inside the plastic cover on the front of my binder. It dictated the events of my day. English and math, Latin and history, I was anxious to get started with them all. I felt great. I was confident. I was ready.

"You're just like your mother, organized and prepared," my

father said. "When I was your age all I wanted to know was what period was lunch and when was gym. You know, Brookie-Love, you look terrific."

"Thanks, Chabadee."

Whenever he called me Brookie-Love, I would call him Chabadee. I knew that he liked it when I called him that.

"Thanks for taking off from work to be with me today," I said.

My dad and I were pals. We understood each other; our personalities were very much the same. It would take only a look or gesture for either one of us to know exactly what the other was thinking. My father would always sing to me his own rendition of Barry Manilow's "I Can't Smile Without You," and I knew it was the truth.

"I wouldn't have missed it for the world," he said, "and, you know, this is the first time that your mother has missed a first day since you guys started school. You know how difficult it was for her to leave this morning and not be here with you."

"I know, she was a little upset before she left, but it's really okay. We'll get a chance to talk when she gets home," I said.

"How do you want to handle the bus stop?" my father asked cautiously. He said it as if he was hoping that I would say what he wanted to hear.

"What do you mean?" I asked, perplexed.

"Do you want to go down there by yourself and I'll wait here? Or do you want me to go with you? Whatever you choose is fine with me. I don't want to embarrass you or anything."

"You won't embarrass me," I answered. "Everyone at the bus stop knows you and it is my first day after all. I'll have plenty of opportunities to walk down there by myself."

"You're not just saying that because you think you might hurt my feelings, are you? Believe me, I understand," he said. "When I was your age, I would never have let Grandma walk me to the bus stop."

"No, really, I want you to come with me," I said.

We walked and we talked and he held my hand. If I had known then that it would be the last time that I would be able to feel his hand in mine, I would have never let go.

JEAN

I HAD GONE TO LUNCH with Chris and Astrid, the girlfriends I had made during the time I did my student teaching. We all went to a fast-food place nearby that was so crowded we had to sit on the curb outside to eat. We didn't mind, though; it was a beautiful day and the fresh air was a welcome change from our hot, stuffy classrooms. It had been a productive morning. After a brief teachers' conference, I set up my classroom and was getting prepared for the next day. I felt confident. I was ready.

Despite my initial apprehension about leaving the kids, I was able to put the normal routines of home behind me. As I chatted with Chris and Astrid, I found that I wasn't worried about the family and felt secure that all was well at home.

Chris, Astrid, and I had just returned from lunch when one of the ladies from the main office stopped us in the middle of the corridor.

"Jean, there's an emergency phone call for you in the nurse's office," she said urgently.

"For me? Who is it?"

"It's Ed, your husband," she answered.

"Did he say what was wrong?" I asked with my heart racing.

"No, just that it was an emergency."

It was as if I had gotten a call at two in the morning, waking me out of a sound sleep. First I was confused and then felt an overwhelming sense of panic. My mind was chasing after all the possibilities of what might be wrong.

"Where's the nurse's office from here?" I said to Chris.

Chris grabbed my hand and pulled me down the hallway. I had a tingly heightened sense of awareness. Everything was louder, but less distinguishable.

"What could be wrong?" I asked Chris. "What could possibly be wrong?" It seemed to take forever to get to the nurse's office.

"Where's the phone!" I yelled when we finally arrived. The noxious smell of rubbing alcohol and antiseptic spray intensified the nausea I was feeling from my undigested fast-food lunch and the news from the impending phone call.

"Here, it's your husband," the school nurse said. For an instant I stopped to try to read the expression on the nurse's face but quickly grabbed the phone.

I paused a moment before I spoke.

"Honey, what's the matter?" I said to Ed. I didn't really want to hear his response.

"There's been an accident," Ed said. He said it calmly, but I was able to detect the nervousness in his voice.

"What? . . . Where? . . . Who?" I said anxiously.

"Brooke has had an accident," Ed responded, his voice beginning to crack. I could tell he was upset. "I need you to come to the Stony Brook emergency room," he said. "Get someone to drive you and come quickly."

That was all I knew until I reached the hospital.

. . .

Ed had taken Reed to Phil's barbershop in Stony Brook Village as he had planned. The village sits on Long Island Sound, just north of where we live. It's beautiful there. It's a central point on Long Island, midway between Brooklyn in the west and Montauk Point in the east. Colonists who came to this area date back to before the Revolutionary War. The cliché "Washington slept here" actually applies to an inn there. The stories about Stony Brook Village are not just historical, though. There are family memories that are just as rich, just as significant. Concerts on the village green in the summer, tree lightings at Christmas in winter, and feeding the ducks all year long on the pond near the gristmill. These memories are a vivid part of our family life.

Reed jumped out of the car and ran ahead while my husband found a spot to park. Phil's barbershop was very crowded; it seemed that all the kids in the neighborhood had waited to the last minute to get their haircuts. Everybody in Stony Brook went to Phil the barber. He is a first-generation Italian who spoke with a pretty heavy Italian accent. Phil liked everybody and everybody liked Phil. He really was the only game in town. Phil had taken on some extra help that day because he knew he would be busy, but the wait was still ridiculously long.

"Business is good, Phil?" Ed asked, not needing an answer given the number of people in the small shop.

"*Va bene, grazie,*" Phil replied. "How is-a you wife? She's such a nice-a lady," Phil said. "She's Italian, right?"

"Oh yeah, she was born in Brooklyn and came out here with her family when she was five. And am I glad she did. She's my Didaseenabopaseech with the meatball eyes," Ed said. "She started a new job today teaching over in the Middle County school district. And Reed's sister Brooke started junior high school today. It's a banner day in the Ellison house."

After about an hour of flipping through outdated magazines, Reed was called to the big, red leather barber chair. He had grown since last year, and he could now see his reflection over the bottles of hair tonic, sprays, and powder.

"Such-a big-a boy," Phil said. "No more booster seat for you. What-a kind-a haircut does a-you boy want?"

"Oh, just clean him up a bit," Ed said. "Not too short and not too long. I guess a regular would be good. His mother likes it short but he doesn't, so kind of split the difference."

Phil began his masterpiece, warming up his scissors by snipping imaginary pieces of hair on the side of Reed's head. Once his scissors made contact, tufts of light brown hair that still showed traces of the summer sun fell haphazardly to the floor. The clicking of Phil's scissors was hypnotic, and my husband's attention slipped alternately between the activity in the shop and the thoughts in his head.

He reflected on how each new school year marked the passage of time and how it seemed to be moving so quickly. He yearned for the days when the kids were all very little but recognized that each phase of life brought with it its own treasures. His emotions were torn between wanting them to remain young and the knowledge that they must continue to grow. The clock on the back wall of the shop caught Ed's eye as he got up from his seat to check Phil's handiwork. It was getting late. Ed began to feel a little anxious; he needed to be home in time to meet Brooke at the bus stop. The bus was due back at one. He knew he couldn't miss the bus after having told me not to worry, that he would be there to meet her. Ed paid the bill, gave Reed money for Phil's tip, and headed toward the parking lot.

"No forget-a you lollipop, and take-a one for you sister, too," Phil said.

It was about twelve-thirty when Ed and Reed left Phil's shop. They passed right by the junior high school on the way home. From the road as they drove by, they could see all the buses lining up. Like a long yellow snake, the buses, each with its own destination, formed a circle in front of the school. As he passed by the red-brick building, Ed thought for a moment that he would stop and pick Brooke up. Again he thought it might embarrass her or that he would appear too overprotective. They drove right by, didn't stop, and went straight home to wait for her there instead.

Kysten was up and dressed and waiting for her father and Reed to get home. Reed went to a friend's house to enjoy his last day of summer freedom. The warmth of the early afternoon sun had replaced the crispness in the morning air. Kysten and Ed decided to wait for Brooke's bus at the end of the driveway. The shade from the sycamore trees that lined the street shielded their eyes from the sun, allowing them to see down Sheppard Lane to the bus stop. Our neighbor Pearl pulled up in her car and stopped to talk. Ed and Pearl were filling each other in on what was going on with the kids and work when the bus arrived. It stopped, but Brooke didn't get off.

"That's strange," Ed said to Kysten. "I thought Brooke was supposed to be on that bus. Could that have been the wrong one?" he questioned.

"I don't know, Dad," Kysten replied. "I think that was the one she was supposed to be on."

"You're waiting for Brooke?" Pearl asked. "I thought school started tomorrow."

"No, she had orientation today," Ed said. "Regular classes start tomorrow."

He looked at Pearl but was now distracted. He really wasn't overly concerned, just confused. Something wasn't right.

"Mr. Ellison! . . . Mr. Ellison!" There was a panicked voice from a distance.

"Who's that running across your front lawn?" Pearl said.

Ed turned around and saw Brooke's friend Elizabeth, who lived up the street, running toward him.

"Mr. Ellison!" Elizabeth cried out again. She was out of breath and had a look on her face that was chilling.

"Mr. Ellison . . . Brooke . . ."

"What is it, Elizabeth, what's wrong?" he said.

"Brooke was hit by a car on Nicolls Road."

"Get in the car!" Pearl shouted.

Ed and Kysten jumped into the backseat of Pearl's car and they sped off down Sheppard Lane to Sycamore Drive, the only street from our development that lead to Nicolls Road. Ed's mind was racing but he wasn't alarmed. He really didn't believe that anything serious had happened. He felt that Elizabeth must have been mistaken. Brooke was supposed to be taking the bus home and, in his mind, couldn't possibly have been on Nicolls Road.

Nicolls Road is a major four-lane highway that runs from Stony Brook on the north shore of Long Island to Patchogue on the south shore. It also separates Murphy Junior High School from our development. Cars on that road travel in excess of fifty-five miles an hour. All the kids had strict instructions to stay away from Nicolls Road.

Pearl's car approached Nicolls Road where the crossing guard usually stands and no one saw anything out of the ordinary. Ed said to himself, "Nothing is going on here, this just must be a cruel joke." As they slowly drove into the intersection, he instinctively looked left, and saw nothing.

"What the hell is this all about? I don't see anything," Ed said.

He then looked to the right. About a quarter mile up the road he saw cars pulled over and an ambulance pulling up. He still didn't believe anything was wrong.

"Pearl," Ed said, "Brooke wouldn't be up there. Why would she be way up there?"

They turned right, and as they got closer Ed saw loose-leaf papers and colored folders strewn all over the highway. Things began to move in slow motion, almost dreamlike. He couldn't catch his breath. It was as if someone had punched him in the stomach

"Oh my God! Oh my God! Oh my God!" Like an incantation, he repeated those words over and over. Pearl pulled the car over onto the side of the road. Ed told Kysten to stay in the car while he and Pearl got out.

"Brookie-Love!" he screamed and ran into the middle of the road. He was grabbed by two EMTs.

"Let me go, that's my daughter. . . . Brookie-Love! I have to see her!"

"You can't go over there," said the EMT in the navy blue jumpsuit, "there's nothing you can do right now."

As Ed watched the chaotic scene before him, the seriousness of the situation unfolded. Police cars pulled up, sirens blaring. Cops and EMTs pushed people out of the way. People were shouting and screaming commands, but nothing was registering in my husband's mind. From the back of the ambulance the EMTs were pulling out equipment. Ed could see Brooke lying on the highway median. The car's impact had thrown her nearly one hundred feet. She was bleeding, had lost consciousness, and her body was completely limp. Two men were administering CPR: a young medical student and a local fire chief had stopped immediately after the accident and had begun resuscitation right away.

On the side of the road was the car that had hit her. The front end and radiator were pushed in and the windshield was broken. Police officers, looking for mechanical problems, poured over it like ants on a sugar cube. Detectives measured the tire skid marks to calculate how fast the car was going. The attention to these details seemed frivolous. Pearl had been trying to find out what had happened.

"Brooke didn't get on the bus," she said to him.

"What do you mean?"

"She decided to walk home," Pearl said.

"Up here?" he said.

"She apparently decided to go with some of her friends," Pearl explained.

They had cut across the playing fields in the back of the school and came onto Nicolls Road through a path in the woods that was used by the older kids. The path came out at a spot where there was a break in the guardrail that made it easier to cross. It was opposite the Christian Science church, whose woods were at the back of our development. It would have been a ten-minute walk. . . . Brooke never made it across.

The EMTs needed to get Brooke to the hospital quickly but not at the expense of risking further injury. No one knew the severity of her wounds at that crucial time. They carefully got her onto a stretcher and into the back of the ambulance. The closing of the ambulance doors had an awful sense of finality to it. Ed wanted to see Brooke, talk to her, touch her. Somehow he felt he might never get that chance again. The rescue squad wouldn't let him go with her.

"They're taking her to University Hospital, Pearl," Ed cried out. "We have to get there before they do." He jumped into the front passenger seat and turned to check on Kysten, who was still sitting in the back.

"It's going to be okay, honey," he said to her.

As though not hearing him and believing the contrary, she cried repeatedly, "I never got to tell her that I loved her. . . . I never got to tell her I loved her."

Stony Brook University Hospital was at the top of the hill, only three minutes away. You could see it from the accident scene. Pearl, honking the car horn, sped past the ambulance and dropped Ed at the emergency room while she parked the car and watched after Kysten. Ed was standing outside the ER doors when the ambulance pulled up and started backing in. The high-pitched beeping sound hammered in his head, signaling not only the vehicle's arrival but also the delivery of its terrifying and trea-sured contents. The doors flew open and the EMTs pulled the stretcher out. Its metal legs unfolded and slammed to the pave-ment. Ed strained to see Brooke; he still couldn't believe it was actually her. The mask that covered her tiny face made it even more difficult. Could that really be her? he thought to himself.

The time that had elapsed from the accident to the hospital didn't change anything. The reality still hadn't set in. Ed then saw the black-and-white outfit and the patent leather shoes that had been so important to Brooke only a few hours earlier. They were now meaningless to the medical staff who stripped them off her. Brooke was being cared for by strangers. Her life was in their hands. "That's my little girl," Ed screamed in his head. "I'm her father!" He felt helpless and frustrated. Someone else was doing his job.

An ER doctor and a nurse stood just outside the Emergency Room doors.

"How does she look?" the ER doctor asked, trying to get a read from the ambulance crew. They didn't say anything. They just shook their heads, sending a very clear message that the situation was a bad one.

"There are multiple injuries, she's not conscious, and she's not breathing on her own. I think we're going to lose her," said one of the EMTs to the doctor and nurse as the stretcher was wheeled passed them.

The ambulance crew must not have realized that Ed was standing there when they made their fatal prognosis. One of the medics recognized him from the accident scene and signaled the nurse that he and Brooke were connected.

"Sir, are you with her?" the nurse asked Ed, putting her hand on his shoulder.

"Yes, I'm her father."

"You need to come with me. I know it's still premature, but you need to prepare yourself. It doesn't look very good right now," she said compassionately.

Ed felt as though he was falling backward, like things were rushing past and he couldn't stop them.

The nurse pulled my husband into one world as Brooke was pushed into another. Ed watched helplessly as the doors of the trauma room swallowed her up.

Chris drove me to the hospital. Neither one of us could figure out what had happened. Ed had just told me to come quickly. As we drove down Nicolls Road we could see that the police had cordoned off the intersection of our development. Somehow I knew it was because of Brooke. Chris pulled up to a cop standing by the wooden sawhorses that had been placed across Nicolls Road.

"You can't go down there," he said. "The road is closed."

"That was my daughter in the accident. I need to get to the hospital," I said, leaning over toward the driver's side window. I don't know how I knew that, I just did.

"What's that, ma'am?" he asked.

I repeated myself and he let us through. We drove past the break in the guardrail across from the Christian Science church. I knew that was the spot.

Doctors streamed in and out of the waiting area, trying to keep Ed and me up to date on what was happening. The medical staff would not let us into the trauma room to see our daughter. There were orthopedic surgeons, neurosurgeons, plastic surgeons, emergency room doctors and nurses, and the chief resident surgeon, who was trying to coordinate what seemed to be chaos.

"Mr. and Mrs. Ellison, I'm the resident surgeon and I've been working on your daughter."

We all shook hands and sat down. Neither one of us could imagine what he was about to say. I searched the doctor's face for some clue but couldn't read him. Ed feared that he was going to tell us that it was over, that Brooke didn't make it.

"Is she alive?" I asked. I was distraught and still dazed from the initial news.

"What's happening to her?" Ed questioned

"Yes, she is alive," the doctor answered. "Your daughter's condition is very serious, however, and she is in a precarious state."

His response seemed clinical and unemotional as though he were describing our daughter's condition to the interns on rounds.

"There's hope," I said. "That's what I really need to hear right now."

I squeezed Ed's hand and we looked at each other, trying to find some answer in each other's eyes. Each of our faces reflected what the other one felt. We were both in a place that we had never been before. The things that go through one's mind at times seem so peculiar. I thought about how lucky we had been. Was this just the balance-in-the-universe theory, where for every good thing there is a corresponding bad thing? Was Brooke's accident just a response to all the good that was happening in our lives?

"I know that this is very difficult for you," the doctor said, "but I want you to know that we are doing everything in our power to help your daughter."

"Can you tell us more specifically . . . what's happened to her and what we should expect?" Ed asked; his forehead creased like it always did when he was concerned. He was trying to be calm more for my sake than anything else.

"The prognosis is not good," the doctor answered. "I can only tell you what we know right now. It appears that she has sustained a skull fracture. She has a broken left leg and her right knee is dislocated. Her arm has been broken, and she has a separated shoulder. She has bitten off the front part of her tongue, and, from what we can determine"—he paused and seemed to look even more serious than he had been—"there might be some brain and spinal cord damage."

"How do you know that?" I demanded.

"She sustained serious injuries to both her head and neck," the doctor said, "and the EEG readings are flat."

"What does that mean?" Ed said

"It means she's not showing much brain activity, and she has had some level of spinal cord damage in the cervical area," he tried to explain.

"Is she paralyzed?" I asked, afraid to hear the answer. "Is she going to know who she is and who we are?"

"It's too early to tell, she's still in a coma," he said.

"Oh my God, honey," I cried to Ed. "I don't know if I can survive this. If she dies, or if she . . ." I couldn't bring myself to say anything more.

Friends, family, and the priests from our parish came to the hospital to sit vigil. Prayers were said for comfort and idle conversation was made to distract everyone from what was really happening. The family pediatrician came up to the hospital to see what he could do to help. He was a friend whom all the kids called by his first name, Richard. He was like a big kid himself and always made them feel comfortable whenever they were sick. He was Ed's friend and running partner.

"I'm sorry. I came as quickly as I could when I heard," Richard said. He gave both of us a hug, pulled up a chair and sat down in front of us.

"You don't know what it means to us to have you here right now," I said. "Richard, nothing seems to make sense anymore. The world has gone mad and I'm going mad along with it," I said.

"Don't think right now," Richard said. "I've found that thinking is terribly overrated."

"They won't let us in to see Brooke," I said desperately. "I need someone who knows her to look at her and tell us honestly what's going on."

"Let me see what I can do," Richard said. "I'm affiliated here and I don't think I'll have a problem."

Throughout the day, Richard went in and out of the trauma room to monitor and interpret what was going on for us. He corroborated everything the other doctors said, but having it come from him made it easier for us to accept.

He pulled no punches and gave it to us straight without a lot of clinical gibberish.

"Brooke's in pretty bad shape," Richard said. "We may lose her, or if she survives it's difficult to say what the outcome will be. . . . Do you want to see her?"

"Can we?" I said apprehensively. I wanted so much to see Brooke, touch her and talk to her, but I was also terrified as to what I might find.

"I think that I can make that happen," Richard said.

Ed and I were finally allowed to go in and see Brooke at about nine that night. We had been there for seven grueling hours, sitting, pacing, and trying to make sense out of what was happening around us. Nothing could have prepared us for this. Richard led us through two large swinging doors into a room lined with tables. It was a place set up to handle catastrophes like airline crashes, where there could be a number of trauma victims. In the middle of the room, at one table, there was activity. Brooke was the only patient in the room. We could see the outline of a tiny body covered in white sheets. Richard walked us over to the table and told the group of doctors, nurses, and technicians that we were Brooke's parents. Richard did the talking.

"She's in a coma and is not aware of what's going on around

her," he said. "She's had a nasty gash to her head on the top of her forehead, that's why her head is bandaged. The tube going into her mouth is connected to a respirator, and that's keeping her alive right now."

I felt weak and nauseous, like I was going to pass out. I had trouble swallowing and couldn't catch my breath. Brooke was barely recognizable. The only part of her that I could see was her face. It was swollen from the impact of hitting the windshield of the car that hit her and scratched from landing and sliding on the pavement.

"Brooke . . . honey . . . can you hear me . . . it's Mommy. I love you," I said.

"We're right here, Brookie-Love, we won't leave you," Ed said.

I moved closer to try to touch her and hug her but couldn't because of all the tubes and monitors that surrounded her.

At about 2:00 A.M., Brooke was taken to the pediatric ICU on the sixteenth floor. Ed and I were no strangers to a hospital setting. I had worked in the dietary department in a local hospital before starting a family and used to visit patients throughout the hospital. Stony Brook Hospital was also familiar to Ed. He was a Eucharistic minister there and gave communion to patients on all the wards. Despite this familiarity, neither one of us was ready to see Brooke hooked up to all the machines, flashing lights, and buzzing alarms. It wasn't natural. It wasn't human.

Day turned to night and night to day and we scarcely knew the difference. No one knew whether Brooke would live or die or, if she lived, what her life would be like. It had been almost twenty-four hours since Brooke's accident, and Ed and I had been at the hospital with her the whole time.

"It's your birthday, sweetheart," Ed said as he leaned over and kissed me on the forehead.

It was September 5 and my thirty-ninth birthday. I looked at Ed and we both shrugged and sighed. I walked over to Brooke's bedside.

"I shouldn't be having a birthday."

"I know that it's not happy, but it's still your day," Ed said. "I have a gift for you at home somewhere . . . that is, if we ever go home."

"The only gift I want is for Brooke to open her eyes and know who I am. I want this all to be over. Nothing else matters . . . nothing," I answered, shaking my head. I hesitated for a moment and then said, "I want so much to be happy. Not because it's my birthday but because I don't want *this*," I said, with a gesture to the walls that made it clear I was not just referring to the hospital room but to everything associated with it. Brooke would always laugh at the way I used my hands when I spoke.

"I don't want to have to understand *this*. I can't process *this*. Nothing makes sense. I want it to be September fourth, not September fifth, not my 'birthday.' I want to go back and start yesterday all over again."

Ed and I were both so tired; we didn't want to think about anything that was going on in that room. We didn't want this horrible situation to be reality. I walked over to the window to look out. From the hospital room, you could see for miles. We were on the sixteenth floor of the tallest building in Suffolk County. There was nothing in the way to block the view. It was ironically majestic. I wanted to be out there, not in here. If I only had wings. Ed walked over and put his arm on my shoulder. He knew what I was thinking and feeling; he thought and felt the same way.

"It's going to be all right," he said. Ed was always saying that, although this time he didn't have the same degree of certainty that he usually did. "I don't know how we're going to get through it, but I know we will. Yesterday, everything seemed so simple, didn't it," he said, "and today . . . I don't know what to think."

"I don't want to think about the terrifying possibilities, but I just can't stop asking myself 'what if?' " I said. "What if she doesn't come out of this? What if she doesn't know us? I'm so frightened, and I have no control over anything. It's out of my hands."

I was used to being in charge, to having a plan for everything. This new situation was so foreign to me. Brooke was lying in a hospital bed, connected to machines, and there was nothing I could do about it.

"I want us to be home," I said. "I want us to be sitting around the dinner table talking about things we thought were important. Silly things. I want everyone to be safe. Remember when the kids were really little and I used to sit in the driveway when they played because I was afraid they would run into the street and maybe get hit . . . hit by a car. . . . It doesn't matter what you do or how hard you try to keep them safe, all it takes is a split second."

It just took an instant and our entire lives changed. What we once thought was secure, what we used to think we could count on, had disappeared. The everyday events of our lives, like tea after dinner, watching a Mets game, or sitting on the deck, seemed eons away. Would it ever be that way again?

I LAY IN BED trying to sleep but my mind didn't extend me that courtesy. I share a bedroom with my older sister, Kysten. We get along okay, but we also fight a lot. There were times when I liked the idea that we shared a room; we could talk late at night if we wanted to. But I kept thinking that it was time I had my own room. After all, I was going into junior high and I should be able to have my privacy. Wouldn't it be neat to have one of those adjustable beds that you see on TV, I thought to myself: the kind that goes up and down and changes the position of your head and feet. I tossed and turned and wondered what school would be like. I thought about everything. I worried about the things all kids worry about at my age. I wondered if I would fit in. Would I be cool, or would I be a nerd? I was going into the honors track at school, which wasn't going to help. There were mostly nerds in the honors classes and I never really felt I belonged there. I didn't see myself as smart, and the honors program seemed a bit too serious for me. When I was in the second grade, we had to take achievement tests and, for some strange reason, I did well. I qualified for an enrichment program, but would have to be bused to another school to be part of it. My parents asked me what I thought and I said I didn't want to leave my friends. We didn't need to talk about it again after that. In the honors program there is a big emphasis on academics and studying. I wasn't sure if that was what I wanted because I'm interested in other things.

I stared at the ceiling and thought that in my eleven years I may not have figured out what our purpose is here, but I have recognized that there is a very distinct difference between boys and girls. I might also add that I am very much interested and curious about that difference. Don't misunderstand me, I love my girlfriends Suzie and Elisa, but boys excite me. I have crushes on a couple of guys. There's Evan in my karate school that I really like, but he doesn't even know I exist. I'm a green belt and he's already a black belt. There's also Thomas from Little League and John Paul from school and church. I think they may like me, too, but I'm not really sure. I never really had a boyfriend. A big part of the excitement of going up to the junior high is the thought that maybe I'll get one.

I started thinking about dancing school. It was starting this week, too. Aside from boys, my biggest passion is music. I love music, all kinds. I play the cello in the school orchestra and I sing in the junior choir at church. I have been going to dancing school since I was two years old. I take tap, ballet, and jazz. I really love to dance. I don't know what I would do if I couldn't sing and dance or play the cello. Dancing is the best. It's better than karate and soccer because moving my body to music satisfies all my senses and stirs my emotions. When I dance with a boy, it doesn't get any better than that.

I was awakened by the sound of a persistent alarm that didn't sound like my clock radio. My eyes opened not to the pink, postered walls and rainbow canopy bed of my room, but rather to white, sterile walls and a railed bed that I had never seen before. The hazy world around me was mysteriously on its side. An IV pole stood before me, suspending bags of blood and clear liquids like a tree bearing fruit. Next to it was another IV pole that was dressed with stuffed animals, so many that they spilled onto the floor. This wasn't my room. Where was I? Hundreds of cards and signs saying "Get Well Soon" covered the walls. Terror ran through my mind as I tried to identify the faces of the people who hovered over me. "What is this horrible place? Who are these people? Why am I not at home?"

My eyes opened again. I didn't remember falling back to sleep or even closing my eyes, but I suppose I must have because most of the strange people were gone. As I stared out into the mess, I slowly became aware of myself. I tasted the blood that was plastered in my mouth and I gagged on my swollen tongue. My head was throbbing, and the alarms and noises in the room made the pain almost intolerable. I tried to concentrate on what was going on around me. My life has changed, I thought to myself, although I didn't know how. I tried to speak, to get some answers, but when I opened my mouth, no words came out. I felt like Ariel in the Disney movie *The Little Mermaid* after her voice had been taken away. There were tubes in my mouth and I felt like I was suffocating. I tried to grab the tubes, but I couldn't move my arms. Am I strapped to the bed? I thought to myself. I tried to sit up but I couldn't. My brain was talking, but my body wasn't listening. My body . . . wait, where is my body? I thought. Why couldn't I feel anything? It felt as though my body was asleep. I tried to sit myself up but found myself restrained by an unidentifiable set of shackles. As if I had been decapitated, I was, in some way, separated from my body.

"Call the doctor, I think she's awake," I heard my father say.

I was lying flat on an object that seemed more like a medieval torture device than a bed, and I couldn't see my parents sitting in the corner of the room.

"Oh, thank God," my mother said.

Before I understood what was happening around me, I was barraged by unfamiliar people.

"Speak slowly," a white-coated man said, "we still don't know how much she will understand."

The comforting sound of my father's voice came from the end of the bed.

"Brookie-Love, sweet pea, can you hear me? We're all here with you."

Flashing a small penlight in each of my eyes, the white-coated man asked me repeatedly, "Brooke, do you know who you are and what has happened to you?

"Brooke, can you hear me? Do you know your name?"

I couldn't answer him, but things became much clearer to me. I didn't really need or want any answers. Somehow I knew. There was a "wushing" sound coming from a big machine next to my bed. It made that sound every time I took a breath. I thought at first that it was counting my breaths, but I realized that it was connected to the tube in my mouth. It was breathing for me. I couldn't move, I couldn't breathe on my own, and I couldn't speak, and no one understood that I knew that. I was terrified. I couldn't answer with my voice, but when I looked into his eyes, he stopped his examination.

"I'll leave you alone for a while," he said, almost as if he had read my mind with his penlight.

JEAN

BROOKE'S BODY HAD BEEN motionless for over thirty-six hours and the doctors' expectations were very grim. They didn't know whether Brooke would come out of her coma, and if she did, there was very little likelihood that she would have any cognitive function. Both possibilities were devastating, but deep down, I never believed that either one would be the case.

Brooke opened her eyes. She couldn't speak but her expression told me what I needed to know. She looked right at me. Her eyes weren't blank or vacant; they were full of questions.

"Brooke, it's Mommy, I love you. Do you know it's me?"

I could see the fear and the sadness in her eyes but I had to know for sure if she understood me.

"Brooke, blink your eyes once if you understand me."

I stared at her and as my heart pounded, she blinked once. It was a hard and deliberate blink that told me she comprehended what I was saying. Tears streamed out of the corners of Brooke's eyes and ran down into her ears.

"Honey, we still have our little girl," I said to Ed, who was standing on the other side of the bed. Ed put his head down on the pillow close to Brooke's face. He started singing softly to her as he had continuously over the past two days.

"Brooke, do you know what happened to you?" he asked. "Blink once for yes and twice for no."

She blinked twice.

"You were hit by a car coming home from Murphy. Do you remember that? Blink once for yes and twice for no."

She blinked twice.

"Do you remember anything?"

She blinked twice.

"You're in Stony Brook Hospital, and everybody here is trying very hard to get you better. You must have a thousand questions and I know that you can't ask them yet, but you will get that chance," I said.

"Your mother and I are here and we're not leaving," Ed said.

"You're not in this alone, we're going to get through this together," I said.

"IT'S TEA TIME." My father looked up from the side of my bed and saw his friend John standing in the doorway. "Tea time," he said again. It was eleven o'clock at night, and just like every night since my accident, John was there with his thermos of hot tea and support.

"Is she sleeping?" John asked.

"No way," my father said. "Brooke and I have been discussing the meaning of life. Actually, I have been doing all the talking and won't let her get a word in edgewise."

"Uh-oh, Brooke, your father's got a captive audience. No one has listened to him in years. I'm surprised he hasn't put you to sleep," John said.

Our eyes brightened when we saw John; we had come to rely on his nightly visits. John was steady and upbeat and always found a way to listen and make us laugh. He and my father were coaches for our Little League team and they became Eucharistic ministers together. He was one of my father's closest friends.

"Eddie, see if you can find some of those Lorna Doone cookie packs so we can dunk them in our tea," John said. "Brooke, I love those Lorna Doone cookies and I think I've made your father a Lorna Doone junkie, too."

My father went across the hall next to the nurses' station, where they had coffee and snacks, scrounged up some packs of Lorna Doones, and came back to the room.

"Where's Jean?" John asked my father.

"She went home for a little while to check on Kysten and Reed and to shower and change her clothes," my father said. "My mother has been staying at the house and taking care of the kids since the accident."

"Yeah, Jackie told me. Your mother is a great lady, Kysten and Reed will be fine."

Jackie is John's wife, and every day both she and our neighbor Mary would come up to the hospital to visit. They would come every day and John would come every night.

"Just taking a shower must feel like a two-week vacation in the Bahamas," John said.

"You know, something like this puts life in a completely different perspective," my father said. "Things that you thought were important become meaningless, and the little things, like taking a shower, are monumental. It makes you realize that you can't take anything in life for granted or waste time worrying about BS."

"Amen to that," John said.

"Brooke, John and I are going out in the hall for a few minutes," my father said. "I'll be able to see you from the doorway. Is that okay with you?"

We were still using the eye-blink communication system. I blinked once for "yes."

Even though I was dependent upon everyone else for nearly everything, I needed time to myself every once in a while as much as I knew my parents did. My heart was breaking but I was reluctant to show it because I didn't want to make things any more difficult than they already were. Time by myself, as rare as it was, and as rare as I wanted it to be, gave me a chance to think about what was happening. It had only been a week since my accident, but I felt like I had changed so much. I was changed physically, there was no denying that, but emotionally and psychologically, I could never return to the girl I was. I was so sure that junior high school was going to change me. I just didn't realize it would happen so fast.

I couldn't believe that while I was in the hospital wondering whether I would live to see the next day, the rest of the world was going on like normal.

"How is that possible?" I asked myself, not really looking for an answer but rather in exasperation and disbelief. "How is it possible that some people can have so much joy when others are facing so much pain?"

It seemed illogical to me. I looked around and saw the ventilator, the suction machine, and the medical supplies, things that just a month before I had never even heard of or thought about but had now become part of my everyday life. Why did this happen?

Other than Richard, my pediatrician, I never thought I would have to see so many doctors. It seemed like they were in my room constantly, which probably wouldn't have been so bad if they weren't so obviously pessimistic. It was almost as if they were afraid of a malpractice suit if they said something positive and it turned out not to be true. There's one doctor who comes in every morning and sticks little pins in me.

He says, over and over, "Ellison, do you feel this?"

He doesn't even know my first name from my last and doesn't understand that I can't answer him. And every day the doctors do their rounds and always discuss me as if I'm not even there. This morning, an orthopedic surgeon was conferring with some residents and interns and discussing the torn ligaments in my knee. My leg was the initial point of impact when I was hit by the car. One of the interns asked the surgeon what effect such extensive damage would have on the function of my leg and if it would require surgical repair. The surgeon said that it was of little consequence because I would have no use of that leg anyway due to my spinal cord injury. I think my father almost lost it completely. He took them out into the hall and told them that if they ever discussed my situation again in front of me, in anything less than an optimistic or positive manner, they would be in need of orthopedic surgeons themselves.

My father isn't the type of man who loses his temper very often. In fact, he always gives people the benefit of the doubt. But this situation was different. He was trying to protect me from more than just the doctors; he wanted to protect me from the world. I was his little girl, and I knew that if he could, he would sooner have given his life than see me in pain.

"Brookie-Love," my father would say with tears in his eyes, "if I could, I would trade places with you in a heartbeat."

"I wouldn't let you, Chabadee," I thought to myself. "I wouldn't let you."

I could see him from my bed, which rotated side to side like a boat in a stormy sea. As the bed moved, my gaze shifted from the cards and signs on the wall of my room, to the hallway where my father and John were talking, and back into the room again. "So *this* is what I had to do," I thought to myself, "to get my own room and the adjustable bed that I wanted."

JEAN

AFTER A WEEK OR SO IN THE ICU, Brooke was still not breathing on her own. The surgeons had to perform a tracheostomy. The breathing tube was removed from her mouth and surgically inserted into her throat. At this point, Brooke could start moving her lips and we could attempt to lip-read. Although it was still very difficult and confusing, communication began to improve. Brooke had so many questions. She was moving her lips but still could not make a sound. I was frantically trying to understand everything she was trying to say.

"Am I . . ." Brooke mouthed.

"Am I?" I repeated.

"Going to . . ." she continued.

"Going to," I repeated.

What did she want to know? Am I going to be able to breathe again? Am I going to be paralyzed? Am I going to die? I was afraid to hear the last part of her question and was sure that I was not going to want to answer it.

"Be left back?" she said.

"Be left back?" I said, surprised.

Of all the questions she could have asked, I was relieved to hear that one. I didn't really know the answer, but my first instinct was to tell her no. I had no experience with something like this and had no idea how long a process it was going to be. Both Ed and I hoped, and felt in our hearts, that she would fully recover. We thought it would be only a matter of time before Brooke would be able to come home and we could resume our lives the way they had been. Brooke would return to her class and I would return to mine.

"Can you promise?" Brooke mouthed again.

How could I promise anything at this point? I didn't know if up was down or down was up, but I would be damned if I wasn't going to be hopeful and positive.

"I promise," I said.

Many of the events that occur in our lives are beyond our control, but not everything. We can take charge of our own attitudes. We can decide whether we are going to be positive or negative. We can view life with hope or with despair. Ed and I decided that, for all of us to survive this, we had to be positive. We had to look for what was good and work with that. Any other approach to this situation would be disastrous for Brooke and the whole family.

My friends Mary and Jackie were angels from heaven. They came to the hospital every day and stayed with us. Jackie and John's son, John Paul, was with Brooke on the day of the accident. He was one of the kids who had decided to walk home that day and not take the bus.

"It could have been John Paul who was hit and not Brooke," Jackie said.

"I know," I said.

"I don't understand. . . . I don't understand why this happened," Jackie said.

"I can't get bogged down in asking why," I responded. "I can't spend the energy searching for an explanation. I just have to find a way to deal with what is. The answer to why will come later and not because I asked. We have to be thankful that it was just Brooke who got hurt and not John Paul or any of the others, also," I said.

We didn't talk about that again.

Until this point, Brooke had been fed intravenously, and none of us, including the doctors, knew whether she would be able to swallow. It depended on how high a spinal cord injury she had. If it had been a C-1 injury, an injury to the first cervical vertebra, she would not be able to eat or swallow.

"When can I eat?" Brooke moved her lips.

"I don't know, but how about right now," I said. "How about something to drink first," I said. "What do you want?"

"A Slurpee."

"What did she say?" Mary asked.

"A Slurpee, from 7-Eleven," I said.

That was all Mary needed to hear. She was gone, out the door and to 7-Eleven and back before we could tell her what flavor. It didn't matter, Mary brought one of every flavor they had.

"What will it be, Brooke: Coke, cherry, or this blue thing?" Mary said.

"Coke," Brooke answered silently but emphatically.

Slurpees come with funny straws that are flat on one end and round at the other. You use the flat end to scoop out the ice. I scooped some ice onto the straw and put a little bit in Brooke's mouth. It was like feeding a baby for the first time. I was scared but excited. I didn't know what to expect. We watched her. She swallowed. We cried and we laughed, we had a victory.

B R O O K E

"HEY, BROOKE, what are you doing, moving up in the world? You have a new room now and a fancy new bed. I turn around for two minutes and you're social climbing."

Lisa, the night nurse, was just coming on to her shift. The nurses that are assigned to me usually work twelve- or sixteen-hour shifts. Many of them are traveling nurses who work all over the country. Lisa was a traveling nurse from California. I liked her because she was young and always had a way of saying the right things. She liked to talk about music and dancing and she didn't ask a lot of questions that I couldn't answer. No one my age was really allowed to come and see me because of the intensity of the situation. So Lisa felt like somebody I could relate to more on a friendship level. They had moved me to another room during the day and had given me a new bed. My new bed still moved from side to side and up and down like my old one, but this one was a little bigger and softer.

"Cool bed, Brooke. I wish I could get one like that," Lisa said.

I wanted to tell her to be careful what she wished for.

"Brooke, I know you must hate this, but I have to do my nursey things."

She took my temperature and my blood pressure. She checked my ventilator, trach, and the IV lines. She examined my leg dressing, my broken arm and shoulder, and my forehead where it had been fractured. I had had plastic surgery on my forehead and the dressing needed to be checked. I was wearing a special cervical collar with a hole in it for my ventilator tube. She examined underneath that, as best she could without moving my neck, to see if I had any sores under it.

"I have to look at your tongue now, Brooke," she said. "I know you hate that, but I have to."

My tongue was so swollen that it filled my whole mouth. It wasn't healing because I kept biting it. Every time I bit it, it would get worse. Our family orthodontist made a bite plate for me to keep me from doing more damage to it. None of the nurses liked to check my tongue because they knew how much it hurt me. How fitting, the only parts of my body where I could feel were killing me.

I always had the feeling that Lisa liked working with me. I didn't get that feeling from all the nurses. I knew I was a hard case. I mean, I was a lot of work and there was so much that had to be done with me. Some of the nurses weren't very nice and would lose their patience. A couple of them were taken off my case. I don't know if they asked to be taken off or if my parents had them taken off. My mother watched everything they did. She watched and she learned.

The days and weeks passed slowly on the sixteenth floor of Stony Brook University Hospital. I was on a ventilator, so I had to remain in pediatric intensive care. There was no television in the room, and for distraction my parents would read to me. They read books and magazines, but mostly books that I would have been required to read in my seventh-grade English class. My mother was already starting to follow through on her promise. As the time drifted away, the circles under my parents' eyes were getting bigger and darker. I felt so much guilt for the pain they were going through. I wanted to comfort them even more than I thought they wanted to comfort me.

Even though my physical condition hadn't changed, I was considered stabilized. There were still times when my blood pressure would drop down to dangerous levels or I would become disconnected from the ventilator and be unable to breathe, but I was not in as fragile a condition as I was when I arrived. My body was making adjustments. My parents still would not take their eyes off me, but now, at the sound of any alarm or buzzer, they could identify the problem and usually fix it. It was a point they never thought they could reach, but they did. I was so proud of them and thankful for what they were doing for me.

"Well, Brooke, it looks like we've done about all that we can here," the doctor in charge of my case said. "It's time for you to move on."

I couldn't imagine what he meant. I had been at Stony Brook University Hospital for six weeks and I couldn't talk, move, or breathe on my own. Where was I going?

"Am I going home?" I asked.

The doctor, who never did get the hang of reading my lips, asked my mother what I said.

"No, honey," my mother said. "Your father and I have to find a rehabilitation center for you. A place where you can get physical therapy and respiratory therapy and where we can get you ready to come home."

"Where will I have to go?" I asked.

"We're not sure yet, your father and I are looking into a few places. There aren't many places that will take a child on a ventilator. We've narrowed it down to two possibilities. There's a rehab hospital in Delaware and one in New Jersey. I think Daddy and I are going to have to go look at the two of them and decide."

I wanted so much to go home. I wanted to be in my own house, in my own room. I wanted to sit at the dinner table and laugh with Reed. I missed Reed so much. I missed my friends.

"How long am I going to be in the hospital?" I wanted to know. "Who's going to be with me? Will I be by myself? Is everybody going to just leave me there and forget all about me? My mother and father have to go back to work; how can they see me if I'm in Delaware or New Jersey? I'm so scared. What if I never get better? What if I never get home?"

My mother and father decided to see both hospitals on the same day. They drove down to Delaware and came back through New Jersey. My mother's friends Mary and Jackie stayed with me while they were gone. Mary stayed with me during the day and Jackie stayed at night. This was the first time my parents weren't with me at the hospital. Mary and Jackie stayed not only to comfort me but to give my mother peace of mind as well.

"Girls' night out, just like a pajama party," Jackie said. "Just you and me, Brooke, hanging out. Next time we do this, though, let's pick a better place. Some places you have to sacrifice the food for the ambience, but truthfully, this place really has nothing going for it. Not even any good-looking guys. Well, maybe there's a couple of good-looking doctors but . . . who was that intern I saw you flirting with yesterday? He wasn't bad."

Jackie was trying to keep everything light. She was trying to distract me because she knew I was scared. She was scared, too, but was doing a great job hiding it.

At about eleven o'clock the phone rang. It was my mother.

"No, why don't you and Ed try to get a decent night's sleep." Jackie was telling them to stay home. "Brooke and I are doing great, right, Brooke?

"Did you decide on a place? Good, now you can put that behind you. You must be exhausted. Get some rest and we'll see you in the morning. Don't worry."

I was dying to know what was going on.

"Looks like the one in New Jersey, Brooke. That's good because it's closer and we'll be able to visit. Your mom and dad will tell you about it tomorrow. They're going to try to get some sleep and maybe we should, too. What do you think?"

I tried my best to smile, but what did I think? I thought that I was going to New Jersey and not going home. I was going to a place where nobody knew me or anything about me. I was terrified. I didn't sleep.

JEAN

IT WAS ABOUT 5:00 A.M. and the light from the hallway was reaching into Brooke's hospital room. As much as I had tried, I didn't get any sleep at all. I had been awake all night thinking about everything that had transpired over the last few days. Columbus Day weekend had just passed, and the smell of autumn had been in the air. It was always one of my favorite times of year. Every year at that time, Ed, the kids, and I would go pumpkin picking out on the east end of Long Island. We would caravan out with his parents, sisters, and all the nieces and nephews. The whole day was spent stopping at farm stands, picking pumpkins and fresh vegetables, and just enjoying each other's company. Then it was back to the house for an autumn festival meal. It was a time that we looked forward to every year, like Christmas and Easter. How different this year was from all the others. Instead of pumpkin picking, Ed and I had to go rehab hunting. It had been a long day of driving down and back from New York to Delaware, and we were exhausted, both physically and emotionally.

"I hope we've made the right choice," I had said to Ed as we drove over the Verrazano-Narrows Bridge on the way home. The water looked so peaceful. We were crossing over a little part of the Atlantic Ocean. I guess you can cross the entire ocean if you did it in little pieces. Maybe that was what our lives were going to be like now, a long journey taken in little pieces.

"Yes, we have, try not to agonize over it," Ed said.

"I want to do the right thing," I said. "The hospital in New Jersey seemed to have sort of a homey atmosphere, didn't it?" I said this not only to convince Ed but also myself. "The staff seemed nice there, and I didn't really feel like we were in a hospital. I think Brooke will like it better there. But . . ." I hesitated and looked back out onto the water. "One of us is going to have to stay with her. We can't leave her there by herself."

"There's no provision for parents at either place. There's no

Ronald McDonald House or any lodging provided by the hospital," Ed said.

"I know, we'll have to rent a room or something. I can't leave her there! I won't leave her there!"

I was getting upset. Every day there was something else to deal with, another problem to solve. The expenses were becoming astronomical. I didn't know whether we were going to lose our house, let alone be able to rent another place in New Jersey, too.

"I never said that we should leave her there by herself," Ed said. "Don't worry, it'll be okay, we'll work it out."

I didn't know what we would do or how it would work. The thought of splitting up the family terrified me. Ed and I hadn't been apart since we were eighteen years old, when he went away to college. Then, after his freshman year, he transferred home to a local college to be with me. We got married in his senior year. We had not been away from each other since. And what about the kids, I thought. What would Kysten and Reed do? Kysten is thirteen and Reed is only nine. What are they going to do without me there? I started to cry. I was afraid for all of us. What we do by choice and what we have to do through necessity very rarely coincide. We called all over looking for a place for me to stay, but we couldn't find anything in time. We had to move Brooke anyway.

Tina, one of the night nurses, quietly peeked her head into Brooke's hospital room as she got ready to do her early-morning rounds. The light from the hall reflected off the stethoscope that hung around her neck. As she tiptoed in, she was surprised to find that I was awake.

"Good morning, Jean. You're awake early. Today's the big day, isn't it?" she whispered.

"Yes, I've been up all night wishing that the morning wouldn't come so quickly," I said.

We were leaving Stony Brook Hospital today and going to rehab in New Jersey. I was apprehensive not only about the trip to a strange place, but also because this would be the first time Brooke had been moved since her accident. Brooke was so medically fragile due to all her injuries that I was afraid any movement would cause more damage. We were told that going to rehab was the logical next step for Brooke and she would begin to make progress there. The doctors said that in rehab she would get respiratory therapy in the hopes of getting her off the ventilator. She was going to get physical and occupational therapy that, we hoped, would result in her regaining the use of her body. We didn't know what to expect and neither did the doctors.

At that time, the medical community had very little experience with injuries like Brooke's because, as the doctors had told us, people usually didn't survive injuries as extensive as hers. It was a miracle that she had. What the doctors did know was that spinal cord injuries were unique to each individual. The best-case scenario, they said, would be that Brooke's spinal cord was just swollen, and once the swelling went down she would begin to recover. At worst, the spinal cord was severed and she would not be able to move or feel anything below the point of injury. All the tests that had been done were inconclusive. It was just a matter of time; we simply had to wait and remain hopeful.

It had been six weeks since Brooke's accident and Stony Brook Hospital was unable to keep her any longer. Before her actual discharge, Brooke had to have her neck stabilized. She had been wearing a cervical collar, but that was not going to be adequate over the long haul. The surgeons put her in a halo brace. Four rods were screwed into her skull, two in the front and two in the back. The rods started well above her head and extended down below her shoulders into a big plastic body jacket. It kept her head fixed in one position, looking forward. It was called a halo brace because there was a ring that circled the top of the head and was attached to the four metal rods. As hideous as this contraption was, it was aptly named in my mind, because she was my angel.

"I'm going to start getting Brooke ready, then," Tina said. "Lisa is going to be helping me, so you should try to rest a little if you can."

I nodded my head, but knew I wouldn't be able to. I wanted to help get Brooke dressed; this was the first time in six weeks that she would be wearing regular clothes. I wanted her to have something normal, to give her a sense of dignity. I picked out some nice clothes that I thought she would feel good in, but because of her bulky halo brace, I had to cut them up the back anyway, just like her hospital gowns. I began to realize that I had to think about everything differently. Even the most basic things that we all take for granted, like getting dressed, had to be thought out in new ways. The first time we washed Brooke's hair, we had to do it while she was in bed, using a washbasin. What would have ordinarily been a five-minute endeavor turned out to be an experience that lasted well over an hour. Along with the dirt and grass and blood that were there because of her accident, large clumps of hair came out. We were told that this was normal, but it was becoming apparent that these new definitions of normal were dramatically different from the ones we were used to. Washing Brooke's hair, brushing her teeth, seemingly insignificant tasks for most people, became monumental milestones and achievements for us. Was this normal?

Making the transition from the hospital to rehab was going to be difficult. Even though the experience at Stony Brook Hospital was terrifying and painful, leaving was not easy. It had become familiar in a strange way. It was close to home and we had grown attached to some of the nurses. None of us knew what to expect in rehab, what would be involved, or how long it would take. Our only hope was that it would help Brooke get better, that she would learn how to breathe on her own and regain the use of her body.

Early on, Ed and I had recognized that much of what was happening was out of our hands. Brooke was still alive, we were coping and managing to make decisions no parent should ever have to make. I began to feel that we were being guided. I felt that if we trusted our instincts and had faith, we would get through this. I felt a divine guidance, an intervention and presence that was realized in the people who entered our lives.

BROOKE

PREPARING TO LEAVE STONY BROOK HOSPITAL, I thought I was going to a place that was simply going to help me get better. A place from which I would quickly leave, not necessarily fully recovered but well on my way to being so. I thought I would soon be able to breathe, sit up, and move around on my own. I thought the doctors and nurses at the new hospital in New Jersey would teach me how to do these things and, by Christmas of that year, I would be home again with my family. After being in Stony

Brook for six weeks, which seemed like an eternity to me, I figured my stay in New Jersey wouldn't be much longer than that. Christmas was the day I envisioned being home, decorating the Christmas tree with Reed and Kysten and opening presents Christmas morning.

Transporting me to the ambulance that was taking me to rehab was scary but exciting. It was the first time I was out of my hospital room in six weeks. I was transferred to a gurney and was able to see for the first time many of the things that had been described to me by visitors and nurses. The nurses' station, which was almost like a bunker when the nurses needed to get out of the trenches, was pretty much how I had envisioned it. Nurses peered out from behind piles of charts and trays of cookies to see me wheel by. The hallway felt and smelled different than I had expected. There was a faint aroma of coffee that reminded me of Sunday mornings at home. It was cooler than my room and I could feel the air against my face as I was wheeled down the hall. It felt like an early spring breeze after a long winter. It was wonderful. Sensory impressions were becoming more and more important to me. What I was able to hear, see, taste, and smell became my sole sources of stimulation and reminders of the way my life used to be. I began storing these images away in my mind so that I could call on them when I needed them.

As we waited for the elevator that would take us down to the ambulance, I began to sense that I was being stared at. There was a little boy, with his mother and father, who was also waiting for the elevator. He seemed transfixed, almost hypnotized by what he saw. He was looking at my halo brace, my ventilator, and the tubes that I was attached to. He was about six years old, half my age, and I couldn't tell if he was scared or just curious. We made eye contact, and he quickly buried his head in his mother's lap.

I wanted so much to say something, but I couldn't talk. I didn't want him to be afraid of me; that would have been too much for me to bear. He turned around again as if compelled to look at something he didn't really want to look at, and I smiled at him. He hesitated, thought for a moment, and smiled back. I'm sure he doesn't know it, but he helped save my life.

Getting into the ambulance, I was able to see the sky and feel the sun on my cheeks for the first time in over a month. I never would have thought something as simple as that could mean so much. We pulled away from the hospital and started to make our way down Nicolls Road. We passed Murphy Junior High and I began to wonder what was going on in there. I wondered what I would have been doing if I had been there, too. It was October 13, a week before my twelfth birthday, and I began to think about my friends, about my brother and sister, and about my life . . .

My birth on October 20, 1978, was a difficult one. I was upside down in utero and had to figure out how to turn myself around before I could make my way into the world. Even then I didn't do things the easy way. It seems I was giving my parents gray hairs from the get-go. My less-than-smooth entrance into the world paved the way for other things early in my life. When I was two months old, right around Christmastime, I contracted pneumonia. We rang in 1979 in the emergency room at our local hospital. The doctor speculated that I was probably allergic to the Christmas evergreens. That was the first and last time I saw a real Christmas tree in the house. I was admitted to the hospital and spent a week there in a little crib with a plastic oxygen tent over it. My parents have said that they stayed up night after night watching me breathe. Maybe that was just a harbinger of things to come.

As a child, I was very curious and inquisitive, and even though intellectual curiosity is healthy, in my case it usually got me in trouble. I was never satisfied with the way things appeared; life, for me, had to be a total sensory experience. I had to touch, taste, and smell everything. After I started walking—at nine months old—my mother would always find me sticking things in my mouth, shoving things in my nose, or with my hands on things that were certainly better left alone. I could be found putting Tupperware bowls on my head, flipping through books on the bathroom floor, or stuck in the wastepaper basket with just my feet hanging over the top. I liked to explore and find new things to do, extend my boundaries and look for answers. Even though my antics often got me into difficult predicaments, I think my parents were usually able to see the humor in them.

My sister, Kysten, however, wasn't quite as entertained as everyone else. She had been the center of attention for over two years and, as is typical of the firstborn, the prospect of sharing center stage never really sat well with her. Growing up, it was clear that Kysten and I were sisters because we looked like sisters. Anyone could tell that we were from the same parents. We would sometimes even dress the same. She has long brown hair like our mother and brown eyes to match. She has a nice smile that usually gets people's attention. For about four years, though, until she was thirteen, she had to wear a molded plastic back brace, like a corset, to help correct a curve in her spine caused by scoliosis. She hated to wear it and I hated that she had to. I was afraid that she was self-conscious and embarrassed by it. The thought of anyone making fun of her upset me. We never really talked about it, but I wish she knew how I felt.

Although we did almost everything together—dancing, soccer, Girl Scouts, karate—we did them in parallel. We were together, but we didn't really share the experiences. I always got the impression that Kysten fancied herself an adult rather than a child, and our ideas of fun were completely different. I liked getting dirty, Kysten liked to dress up. I liked spontaneity; she preferred a routine. We were different, but I wish that we had had more respect for each other's differences. Maybe then we could have better appreciated our time together. I know that I loved her and she loved me, but it wasn't always clear how much we really understood each other.

My brother, Reed, was born in June of 1980. With his arrival, the yellow Cape Cod house that we first lived in proved to be too small. Kysten, Reed, and I were all sharing one bedroom, and it was beginning to get a little too crowded. In the summer of 1981 we moved to a bigger house in Stony Brook, farther east on Long Island. My parents chose Stony Brook because of its excellent school district. Our education was always very important to them. Stony Brook was also a much quieter area, with less traffic and congestion. It seemed a safer area for us to grow up in and they felt fortunate to find a house they could afford and that better suited our needs.

Everyone was happy with our move to Stony Brook. We had a grassy backyard where Kysten, Reed, and I could run around and play. My father built a swing set for us and he hung a tire from one of the maple trees in the yard. I used to love to climb into the tire and push myself higher and higher, faster and faster, until I could lean way back and watch the sky rush by. I felt free, like I was flying, like I was an eagle. I could do that forever.

When Reed was born, I gained not only a brother but also a friend—not just any friend, but the kind that almost becomes a part of you. We were inseparable. We were as close as twins. The fact that we were siblings, however, didn't stop the very strong maternal instinct that I felt toward him. I watched out for Reed, and he didn't seem to mind my doting on him. I always worried that something bad might happen to my brother, and those thoughts frightened me.

When Reed was little, he had a round face with chubby cheeks and a buster brown haircut that outlined his big hazel eyes. He always wore denim overalls with the straps sliding off his shoulders. He had a giggle that was infectious, and once he got going he would often laugh so hard that he would fall out of his chair. While Kysten and I went to dancing school, Reed studied the piano. He started taking lessons when he was five years old. He got pretty good and his playing proved to be an outlet for him and a source of enjoyment for the entire family. I loved to listen to him play.

I was thinking about my sister and brother more closely. I thought about how much I loved them and when I would be able to see them again. As the ambulance drove passed the entrance to my development, I wanted to tell the driver to turn and take me home. I wanted to see Kysten and tell her all the things that I hadn't said. I wanted to be with Reed. I missed him so much and I knew he missed me, too. I wanted to hear him laugh and I wanted him to play the piano for me. I felt like a captive. I was being taken to a place where I didn't want to go and there was absolutely nothing I could do about it. I just wanted to go home.

ED FOLLOWED THE AMBULANCE in the family car and we all arrived at the rehabilitation hospital some time after noon. The hospital's appearance was deceiving from the outside. It was set in a residential area and blended nicely into the community. If you weren't looking for it, you could easily pass right by without even noticing it was there. As is the case with most places, the first thing we all noticed when we entered through the large sliding doors was the smell. It wasn't a bad smell, but it definitely gave you the message that it wasn't a place you would want to call home. It was institutional; a smell that quickly became associated with rehab.

The only thing Brooke could see, as the gurney wheeled her down the hall to her room, was the ceiling as it passed over her. She was lying flat on her back and the halo brace kept her head and neck immobile. It was probably for the best, though, because she couldn't see the children sitting in front of the nurses' station, some of them seemingly frozen, like gargoyles sculpted with expressionless faces. Three other girls occupied the room with Brooke and she was given the bed by the window. It had just become available and I thought about all the patients who had been in that bed before. Had they gone home or had they . . . I stopped, and realized that I really didn't need to know all the details.

"Hey, this isn't bad," Ed said to Brooke as he looked out the window. "There's a beautiful maple tree right outside here, and its leaves are starting to change color. Brooke, maples are the most beautiful trees. Its bright yellow and red leaves will fill the window before long. It will almost be like looking out into our own backyard." Ed spoke as convincingly as he could, but Brooke and I knew that he was grabbing for anything that might help make this transition easier.

The room was painted yellow with dark brown molding. There was a television in the back of the room that, from its position on the wall and the angle of her bed, Brooke was unable to see. Brooke's cousins, Tracy and Kelly, made her a collage of family pictures to hang over her bed so she could have family around her all the time. Ed brought posters from Brooke's room at the house to try to give her a feeling of home. He also brought a painting that was made for her while she was at Stony Brook Hospital. It was painted by a man who called himself "Wheels" and who was serving time in prison. He had been dedicating much of his time in jail to trying to bring happiness to children in hospitals. The picture was of a girl kneeling by her bed and praying; above her head it said "God Bless Brooke." People seemed to come into our lives from the oddest places, but at the times when we most needed them. Wheels was one of those people.

"What do you think, Brooke? This isn't bad," I said.

I was trying to be as positive as possible, but I hated it there. I was scared, but I didn't want Brooke to get any sense of how I really felt. I didn't know how long we would have to stay there, but the thought of just one day was almost more than I could bear. I started to get Brooke unpacked. She had a wardrobe closet with drawers in it for her clothes and a bedside table for her personal items. The space was small, and with four girls in the room, it seemed crowded.

"This is going to be home for us for a while, Brooke," I said. "We're going to have to try to make the most of it."

That first day, the medical director of the hospital and the nursing supervisor came in to meet us.

"How long do you think Brooke will have to stay here," Ed asked, "and when can we start discharge planning?"

"With injuries as serious as your daughter's," the director said, "you can expect her to be here at least a year, very possibly longer."

Ed and I looked at each other and then at Brooke. We were all stunned.

"What?" I said. "That's not going to happen."

"Absolutely not," Ed said. "Brooke, you'll be home sooner than that. Don't worry, sweetheart."

I think, at that point, neither the hospital director nor the nursing supervisor knew what to make of us. I don't know whether they thought we were just naive, stupid, or both, but they made it very clear to us from the expressions on their faces that we didn't know what we were talking about. The fact of the matter was, they were right. We really didn't know what we were talking about. We had no experience with this and we were breaking new ground every day. What if she did have to stay for a year or more, could I endure that? I told Kysten and Reed, when I said good-bye to them, that I would be home as soon as I could. Would it be fair to them to be away for that long? Could I survive that? I had no answers, and realized that decisions about our lives were being made by people we didn't even know. What I did know, however, was that if there was any way humanly possible to get Brooke home faster than that, we were going to do it. Whatever it was, whatever it would take, we were going to try and make it happen.

As nighttime approached we were becoming increasingly more concerned about our sleeping arrangements. We certainly knew where Brooke was going to be staying, but my situation was far from resolved. We were still trying to find a place for me to live in the area and we were prepared to spend the night in the car if we had to. We had hoped to be able to stay at Brooke's bedside that first night.

"Mr. and Mrs. Ellison, you are going to have to leave now," one of the night nurses said. "Parents are not allowed to stay past ten o'clock."

"We really don't have a place to go to tonight," I said, "and we don't want to leave Brooke alone on her first night."

"We don't have accommodations for parents," she said, "and you can't stay here in the room. I'll see what I can find out for you."

When she came back, she said that the hospital was able to make arrangements for Ed and me to stay for the night in one of the unoccupied rooms on the second floor. It was the first time since her accident that Brooke would not have someone with her at her bedside. She was terrified, crying, but was unable to make a sound. We were leaving her there alone in a strange place with people who knew nothing about her. We were all terrified. I came down a few times during the course of the night to check on her. None of us slept at all that first night.

BROOKE

"HI, BROOKE, I'M LINDA. I'll be taking care of you while you're here."

Linda would be my primary nurse, and I met her the first morning I was at rehab. She worked the 7:00 A.M. to 3:00 P.M. shift, Monday through Friday.

"I was telling your parents, Brooke, that I do things pretty much by the numbers. It's important that we stick to a schedule and develop a routine so we can get everything done."

My parents had come down earlier from the second floor and had met Linda before her shift had started. "By the numbers . . . develop a routine," I thought to myself; my mother is going to love her. I had no idea, though, what the "numbers" or "the routine" were going to be.

Linda was a middle-aged woman, probably in her late forties or early fifties. She had salt-and-pepper hair, more salt than pepper, that she kept short, I think, so it wouldn't interfere with her work. She wore glasses with big red frames, almost like yuppie frames, that contrasted with her deep blue eyes. She was intense and every task was accomplished quickly but methodically. She wore a stethoscope around her neck that swung back and forth like a metronome keeping time to her every movement. Linda was experienced and professional, and it was obvious that she knew what she was doing. I think my parents felt confident in her abilities and comfortable that she would be working with me.

"Every morning, you will take your medications and we'll check your vital signs," Linda said. "We'll take your temperature, your blood pressure, and check your oxygen levels. You'll have to urinate, move your bowels, and then get washed up. You'll get a bed bath every other day, and three times a week you'll go in the Hubbard tank."

I think my mother could see the panic in my eyes, or maybe she was just getting a little frightened herself when she asked, "What's a Hubbard tank?"

"It's like a bathtub that we will lift Brooke in and out of," Linda said.

"Oh," my mother said somewhat matter-of-factly, trying not to show that she was scared to death.

"You'll get therapies every day—physical, occupational, and recreational."

"What about schoolwork," my mother asked. "Will there be any time for that?"

"Some of the kids get some schoolwork, but most of our patients have head injuries and are taught basic life skills," Linda said. "It's very rudimentary, but I'm sure that they can get something started for Brooke if she really feels up to it."

"When can we start getting Brooke up out of bed and weaning her off the ventilator?" my father asked.

"We'll be getting her out of bed very soon. About the ventilator," Linda hesitated, looked down without making eye contact, "you're going to have to talk to the respiratory therapist about that.

"Have you met any of the girls in the room yet, Brooke?" Linda asked, I think trying to change the subject.

I couldn't speak or move my head, so my mother jumped in.

"No, she hasn't, Linda," my mother replied for me.

"Then let's see what we can do about that," Linda said.

"Girls," Linda called across the room. "I want you to meet someone. Brooke, meet Keisha, Donna, and Lara," Linda said.

Keisha, who had the bed across from me, was already up and in her wheelchair. She was only ten years old but easily looked twice her age. She was big and had already started to develop into a woman. Her hair was coarse and wiry and it stuck straight up like Don King's, the fight promoter. Everyone in the hospital, including the nurses, was afraid of Keisha. She came from the inner city, where she had been shot and left paralyzed from the waist down. I never found out all the details of how and why she got shot, but felt that it was probably better that I never knew. Keisha was clearly the toughest person I had ever met. She wore a scowl on her face and she could stare anyone down. If she didn't want to do something, she didn't do it. When we met, I smiled at her, and for some inexplicable reason, maybe pity for someone she thought was in a worse situation than her own, Keisha looked back at me and smiled—not a broad smile, but a cautious one, more with her eyes than with her mouth. We had come from two completely different worlds, but our individual misfortunes had drawn us together. I saw past her scowl and she saw past my halo brace. I knew that we would become friends.

Donna was in the bed next to me, on my right. She was several years older than I was, but due to a brain injury from a severe asthma attack, she functioned at a low level. No one could ever predict what Donna was about to do; everything she did was completely unexpected and often without any apparent purpose. Sometimes she would be in the corner tying her shoes together, wearing different color socks, and I remember her once wearing her underwear on the outside of her clothes. Because of her condition, Donna basically had no inhibitions. Out of nowhere, sometimes in the middle of the night or often when she was in the bathroom, Donna would start singing at the top of her lungs. It was usually a song of her own creation or it would be her own unique and often nonsensical rendition of a popular song.

In the bed diagonally across from me next to the door was Lara. Lara was a tiny six-year-old who, in her short life, had already had quite a difficult time. She had a very supportive family but her mother was no longer alive. Lara's injuries were very similar to my own; she had a high-level spinal cord injury, which left her paralyzed from the neck down and on a ventilator. Lara had arrived at the hospital just a few weeks prior to my own arrival. People would often say that Lara and I looked like sisters.

We both had long brown hair and similar features. I always feared, though, that people thought we looked alike because of our similar circumstances. I didn't want to be identified by that. Lara and I had a bond that was created from a common experience I wish neither one of us had ever had. We understood each other and we developed a very unique relationship, one that could only have been formed by a shared experience.

My mother kept an eye on all the kids, especially the ones in my room. That small room with four beds was our community. We were different but, oh, so much the same. We weren't the same age, size, or color, but we had been drawn together by inexplicable forces that had twisted each of our lives. The four of us inhabiting that room became a family, and my mother was at its head. She was with all of us every day until late into the night. Lara called my mother "Mom," and I know that Keisha and Donna felt the same. She would help them and listen to them without documenting everything they said or did in a chart. I don't think anyone would have thought that my mother's first real teaching job would be right there, in that room. She was my mother and my teacher, but I could share her because I knew how lucky I was.

JEAN

AT THE END OF THE FIRST WEEK AT REHAB, Ed was going to have to go home and return to work. Ed's cousin Richie had come up and visited us on the second day that we were there. It was so nice to see a familiar face in such an unfamiliar place. He and his wife, Miriam, and their two daughters, Lisa and Denise, lived in Edison, New Jersey, just one town over from the hospital.

He wanted to know if there was anything he could do to help out. Ed asked him if he knew of a place in the area where I could stay at night. He said yes, he knew of a real nice place, his house. He said that Lisa was away at college and I could stay in her room if I wanted to. Richie, Miriam, and their family, like the boy for Brooke at the elevator in Stony Brook, helped save my life. They accepted me without question or discussion, with loving open arms.

"One, two, three . . . lift," Connie said as she held Brooke's upper body while Linda held her legs and Ed moved her ventilator and guided her tubing.

Connie was Brooke's daytime aide who helped Linda get Brooke ready in the morning. Connie was great, always full of energy, and both Brooke and I grew very close to her. She loved to braid Brooke's hair and paint her fingernails, and because she had young kids of her own, she could talk about and relate to things that Brooke understood. She really treated Brooke as if she were one of her own.

We lifted Brooke into a "geri" chair, a huge pink-colored thing that was primarily used for geriatric patients and looked very much like a dentist's chair on wheels. It had a shelf on the back for a portable ventilator. It was the first time Brooke was in a chair since her accident, and it happened the first week we were in rehab. We saw promising changes during that first week and thought they were just the beginning of much bigger and more significant changes in Brooke's physical condition. Since the day of her accident, Brooke's breathing had been supplemented by oxygen. During that first week in rehab, the respiratory therapists were able to wean her off the oxygen completely. Getting Brooke off the ventilator was our number one concern. Her being tethered to a machine for her every breath was terrifying to all of us.

We thought that removing the oxygen was the first step to getting her off the ventilator totally.

"When can we start weaning Brooke off the ventilator?" I asked the respiratory therapist when he arrived to change Brooke's ventilator tubing.

"We'll be working on that," he said, but in a way that seemed to indicate that it was not as high on his list of priorities as it was on mine.

"What do you think about trying to speak, Brooke?" he asked, in a way that I couldn't tell whether he was just making conversation or whether he knew something that I didn't know.

"What?" Ed said, not really sure of what he had just heard.

"Would you like to speak, Brooke?" he asked again, pulling a small circular piece of blue plastic out of his pocket and holding it up for us all to see.

"What's that?" I asked.

"It's a Passy-Muir," he said.

"A what?" Ed asked again, not really understanding what he was saying.

"It's a Passy-Muir valve. We can put it in Brooke's ventilator tube to redirect her exhaled air over her vocal cords, and as a result, allow her to speak. Would you like to try it, Brooke?" he said.

Brooke, in excited disbelief, moved her lips and said, "Yes."

"How does it feel?" I said, after the respiratory therapist fit it in her tube.

Brooke stared back and didn't say anything. She looked scared and confused as if she had forgotten how to speak.

"Brookie-Love, can you say something?" Ed said anxiously.

After a long pause, Brooke said: "This . . . feels . . . weird," in a raspy, breathy voice.

She wasn't used to how it worked, so each word she spoke came out slowly, separated by a breath or two from her ventilator. Ed and I looked at each other and started to cry.

"I . . . sound . . . that . . . bad?" she said in the same raspy, staccato voice when she saw us crying.

"Oh my God, no," I said. "It's the most beautiful sound I've ever heard."

"This feels weird," Ed said, sensing that Brooke might be upset over the sound of her voice and trying to lighten things up a bit. "Was that all you could come up with?" he said. "How about something like . . . 'One small step for man,' or . . . 'Ask not what your country can do for you.' 'This feels weird,' great line, Brooke," Ed said sarcastically.

Brooke could leave the valve in for only a few hours a day and it had to be out when she ate and slept, but it was a beginning. A beautiful beginning. It was the first time in nearly two months that I had heard Brooke's voice. It was different, but it was hers. There was so much that we needed to talk about together. No more lip-reading or mind-reading to figure out what she needed or wanted. It was a giant step, maybe not for mankind, but certainly for her and for me.

BROOKE

FOR THE MOST PART, my world was four walls, four beds, and one window that reminded me of another life in another time. At times I felt like a prisoner, incarcerated for crimes I didn't know I had committed. Time was passing, but passing slowly. The days were long and the nights were longer.

"Your mother's home, Brooke!" the night nurse shouted into my room from the nurses' station.

My mother would have to leave the hospital every night at about ten o'clock and go back to Richie and Miriam's house. I hated when she had to leave and worried about her getting there safely. Every night, I insisted that she call the nurses' station to tell me that she had gotten home all right. I don't think the night nurses liked that very much, but I didn't care. With the exception of one male night nurse named John, the night nursing staff was different from the other shifts. For the most part they were impatient and intolerant. I thought it ironic that the time I really needed the nurses the most, they weren't there, and even worse, I was afraid of them.

The nighttime was the worst. It didn't matter how long I was there, I was terrified every night. I was afraid to close my eyes because I wasn't sure whether I would get to see the next day. I couldn't have my Passy-Muir valve in at night, so I still couldn't speak or get anyone's attention if something was wrong. If I became disconnected from the ventilator, I had to hope and pray that someone would hear it and then be able to get to me in time. I would try to force myself to stay awake, which made me think about everything. Thinking was all I could do. I was trapped inside my own head. I remembered my father telling me what Richard, my pediatrician, had said about thinking, that it was overrated. I was beginning to understand what he meant.

I lay in my bed thinking about everything that was going on, and everything that I had lost. I missed everyone so much and wanted so desperately to be home. I felt so much guilt for having split up my family and how difficult it was for them. I stared into the darkness and wondered what my life would have been like had I not gotten into this accident. How could I have let this happen? How stupid I was, how careless. I wondered what my friends were doing and whether they had forgotten about me. I wondered whether I would ever see them again and whether I would ever have a boyfriend or a family of my own. I thought about how I should be dancing, tying the ribbons of my ballet slippers around my ankles. I missed dancing so much; I missed moving so much. I stared at the outline of my hand underneath the blanket and strained to get it to move. It wouldn't and I cried. When I cried, I couldn't make a sound, wipe my eyes or my nose. What was this all about? I wanted an answer, an explanation for what was going on and a time line for when it would end. This was not my life. I was supposed to be at school. I was supposed to be a dancer. Why was this happening to me and to the other girls in my room? As I looked around, I wondered what we had all done to deserve this.

All these thoughts raced through my mind without end. Even though I wanted them to stop, thinking about them kept me awake and brought me to a place with which I was familiar. I didn't want to understand the ventilator, the hospital bed, the nurses, the therapies, any of the things that were so terrifyingly different. I wanted my life back. I wanted it back desperately. I cried. I cried for hours, from the dead of the night until I could see the sun come up over the maple tree outside my window.

JEAN

AS IS THE CASE IN MOST HOUSEHOLDS, the passage of time is usually marked by birthdays and holidays. So, too, in rehab. Brooke's twelfth birthday came a week after she arrived in New

Jersey and passed with significantly less fanfare than would have ordinarily been the case. Birthdays at Brooke's age usually involved parties with friends, bubble gum corsages at school, and lots of excitement and attention from friends and family. We were going to have a party for Brooke on the weekend. Ed was going to come with Kysten and Reed. His sisters Amy and Margaret, Margaret's husband, Lee, and her four kids, Christopher, Tracy, Kelly, and P.J., were planning to come, too. We would try to be as festive as possible, but under the circumstances, it was not the way any of us wanted to celebrate. Brooke was grateful that everyone was coming but she was definitely not happy.

"Wait a minute, Reed, slow down!"

I could hear Ed's voice from the hallway.

"Hi, Mom, happy birthday, Brookie," Reed was shouting as he ran into the room.

"Hi, sweetheart, I missed you so much," I said.

"I missed you guys, too," he said.

"Where's Kysten?" I said.

"She's with Dad, they're coming down the hall."

"I think you grew an inch since I saw you last week," I said. "Grandma must be feeding you pretty well."

"Yeah, she is."

"Is everything okay at home, how's school going?" I asked.

"It's okay. Brookie, I learned a new song for your birthday!"

"You did!" Brooke said. She was much more comfortable with the Passy-Muir and was speaking much better with it. "Which one?" she asked.

"It's a surprise," Reed said. "I want to play it for you."

As soon as Monday came Brooke and I would start counting down the days until the weekend. On Saturday mornings Ed would drive from our house in Stony Brook to New Jersey to visit. He would bring Kysten and Reed and they would spend the entire day with us, sleep at Richie and Miriam's house at night, and then come back on Sunday morning and stay until late in the afternoon. We lived from weekend to weekend and we couldn't wait for them to come.

"Hi, Mom," Kysten said as she came into the room with Ed.

She kissed me, gave me a hug, and walked over to wish Brooke a happy birthday. Something didn't seem right.

Ed and I hugged and I didn't want to let go. There was just too much time between hugs and I wanted each one to last as long as it could.

"How're things at home," I asked Ed.

"Everything is fine," he said as he walked over to Brooke. "Hey, Birthday Girl, I heard this great joke, don't let me forget to tell you before I go."

Everything was always fine, even if it wasn't. He never wanted to give me anything else to worry about and I knew he was trying to deflect the conversation.

"How's your mother?" I asked.

"She's holding down the fort," he said.

"I don't know what I would have done without her," I said.

"I know, honey, don't worry," Ed said. I hugged him again.

My mother-in-law had been staying at our house since the accident and went home only on the weekends when Ed brought the kids to New Jersey. She got Kysten and Reed off to school and she was there when they got home. She gave me some peace of mind in an impossible situation. I pulled Ed over to the side of the room and asked him how Kysten was doing.

"She's okay," he said

"No, really, tell me. She doesn't look right, I know some-thing's wrong."

"She's sad, and she's frightened," he said. "She's having a hard time dealing with this. She misses you and she misses Brooke but feels guilty because she really doesn't want to come here. She hates it here. She hates to see Brooke like this, and this place scares her."

"Has she gone back to dancing school yet?" I asked.

"No, she hasn't and says she's not going to," Ed said. "Neither one of them have gone back to karate either."

"Why not?"

"They don't want to go back without Brooke."

"Mom." Reed came over and was pulling on my arm. "Can we go down to the day room, and can I push Brooke down there in her chair? I want to play my new song for her."

"Sure, honey, let's go. It's more comfortable down there anyway."

We would always go into the day room that overlooked a small courtyard and had couches, tables, and chairs in it. There was a piano in there, too, and Reed would always play for Brooke. It was a beat-up old spinet that was never really tuned properly and was always locked.

"Is someone going to steal the piano keys?" Ed asked with a smirk.

"Don't worry, Dad, I can do it," Reed said, and proceeded to take a paper clip from his pocket and unlock the piano.

"What are you teaching him when I'm not there?" I said to Ed.

"I had nothing to do with this one," Ed said with just a touch of guilt on his face.

Ed pushed Brooke's chair closer to the piano and we all pulled chairs around to hear Reed play.

"The piano's not tuned very well and I didn't have a lot of time to . . ."

"Reed, just play," Ed interrupted, "and don't worry about it."

Reed started to play and to sing very softly under his breath. He never sang when he played, but for his sister's birthday he sang the words to "Somewhere Out There" to let her know how much he missed her.

None of us made it through the first stanza. We all kind of looked at each other with tears in our eyes. When Reed finished, there was just silence.

"Hey, Brooke," Ed said, after a long pause, "a duck walks into a pharmacy and says to the pharmacist, 'Give me some Chap Stick and put it on my bill.' "

Thanksgiving came quickly after that and none of us knew what we were going to do. I always loved to bake and prepare for Thanksgiving, and the holiday was always spent with family— grandparents, aunts, uncles, and cousins. We certainly couldn't ask everyone to drive to New Jersey and spend Thanksgiving in the hospital. Almost all of the other children in the hospital with Brooke were able to go home, at least for the day, but because of the extent of Brooke's injuries, and the distance we were from home, we couldn't leave. Ed and I thought we would probably get some take-out food and the five of us would eat it in Brooke's hospital room. It wouldn't be traditional, but we would all be together.

Ed, Kysten, and Reed came to New Jersey the day before Thanksgiving and stayed at Richie and Miriam's. Thanksgiving morning Ed's cousin Richie told him that he and Miriam would be coming up to the hospital in the afternoon. Brooke watched the Thanksgiving Day Parade with Reed, like they always did, while Ed and I thought about dinner. At around two o'clock in the afternoon, Richie and Miriam came by. What we thought was going to be just a short visit turned out to be much, much more.

"Where do we eat and when do we eat it?" Richie said.

"What?" Ed asked.

"You heard me," Richie said. "I don't know about you, but I'm starving."

Richie, Miriam, Lisa, and Denise brought with them an entire Thanksgiving dinner. They had made lasagna, turkey, stuffing, mashed potatoes, vegetables, bread, pies, cookies, everything we could have possibly imagined for a Thanksgiving meal. They also brought with them fancy linens and dinnerware. Most important, though, they brought with them their love and their readiness to spend the holiday with us. None of us were expecting anything like this at all. They were like angels. We set up tables and chairs in the day room and we ate everything. We talked, told stories, Reed played the piano, and, even though we were surrounded by a hospital, we were most thankful. As much as we would have wanted to be home, it was the most beautiful, most heartfelt Thanksgiving we had ever had.

BROOKE

I HAD COME TO THE REALIZATION that I was going to have to spend Christmas and the entire holiday season in the hospital. Christmas was always the deadline that I gave myself to be back home. This was a realization that did not come easily. As much as I wanted to be home all the time, I particularly wanted to be home for Christmas.

As December progressed, it was becoming more obvious that

my recovery was not going to happen as I had hoped. After the big changes that occurred during the first week, things hit a plateau. I came to the understanding that I was not going to be able to just walk out of the hospital or even make significant physical strides. It seemed like rehab was more of a place where I would just learn how to adapt to my new physical condition. It was a long layover between Stony Brook Hospital and going back home.

It was becoming clear that I was probably going home in a power wheelchair like the one I was learning how to use in the hospital. I was probably still going to be on a ventilator. Many attempts had been made to get me off the ventilator; none were successful. I couldn't initiate breaths on my own. There was no message being sent from my brain to my diaphragm. I was probably still not going to be able to move my arms or legs. I was probably still going to be paralyzed. How different this would be from any life I had known.

For the first eleven years of my life I played baseball and soccer. I was a dancer for nine years, studying tap, jazz, and ballet. I played the cello and sang in the church choir. I studied karate and attained a green belt. Each night of the week was designated to some activity, and that's what seemed normal, that was the way life was supposed to be. All the things I did and loved, in my mind, shaped me as a person and established my identity. I was a dancer, I was a singer, I was a cellist. Then, in one instant, my life changed completely.

I could no longer dance or play the cello or hit a baseball. The things I thought defined me were gone. It seemed as though everything from the sound of my voice to the way I got around was different and strange. I wondered if this was a situation I could ever get used to. If the aspects of my life that I thought identified me as a person were no longer there, who was I and how was I to understand myself? This situation was difficult for both me and my parents to come to terms with. It was the outcome that we had most feared but also one that we knew we might have to accept. The thought of Christmas coming just made it much more difficult.

One day in December when I was on my way back to my room from physical therapy, and feeling particularly down, I saw that there was a big Christmas tree next to the door. There were boxes of ornaments and tinsel on the ground around the tree. The therapy departments were organizing a big tree-decorating evening, with holiday cookies, candy, and a carol sing-along. Seeing it made me really think about Christmas, my memories and my traditions.

So much of Christmas is made of Christmases past. Images of Christmases gone by fill our heads like the smell of baked apples and cinnamon fill a warm and cozy kitchen. Tradition and Christmas are as interwoven as the stitching in a needlepoint. Each year, sights, sounds, and smells create a sensory Christmas potpourri. As predictable as Christmas morning following Christmas Eve, we come to expect each Christmas to be what we have known it to be in the past.

Memories and traditions are very important, but they're like two-sided coins. On one side, they give us something to cling to, but on the other side, if they're taken away, we can feel lost.

I was relying on my memories, and felt that without my traditions, my Christmas would have no meaning. I was thinking of my past, and felt that without the use of my body, my life would have no purpose. I was wrong. Before I could go on with my life, I had to learn what it was about myself that was truly me.

I had memories, which could never be taken away from me, and my accident did not rob me of my ability to think, reason, and love. My body would not respond, but my mind and my heart were just the same as they had always been. That was who I was. I would be unable to experience all the things that I wanted, but I still had the most important things—my life and the love of my family and friends, which are the framework on which all tradition is built. My family would be with me on Christmas Eve and on Christmas Day, and I knew then that my life would go on.

JEAN

WATCHING BROOKE STRUGGLE unsuccessfully to try to regain the use of her body and to get off the ventilator was devastating to all of us. We needed to change our plan for the short run while remaining hopeful over the long haul. If no further progress could be made in rehab, we needed to focus on getting Brooke home and getting on with our lives. Hope was critical. Hope was essential for making this work. It was what had gotten us through to this point, and Ed and I both believed that hope not only had psychological ramifications but biological implications as well. We felt that if we had hope, anything was possible. Rehab, though, was not always its best breeding ground. There was an attitude by some of the staff that positive thinking and planning for the future were unrealistic.

"You don't want to give Brooke 'false hope,' Mrs. Ellison, when you tell her that she can do anything she puts her mind to," I would hear all too often.

"There is no such thing as 'false hope,' " I'd say. "False hope is an oxymoron, a contradiction in terms. Either you have hope or you don't."

We needed to stay positive and we needed to stay hopeful and we needed to get the family back together again. I had made a promise to Brooke that she would return to school in September to be with her class. That was a promise I intended to keep. I had made sure that she kept up with her studies while she was in the hospital. I had all of Brooke's teachers from Murphy send her textbooks and a basic plan of study so that she could keep relatively in pace with her classmates. Brooke would be just beginning her first year of Latin, algebra, and physical science, subjects that had never been taught at the hospital before. She had class every day, both in the morning and afternoon. She was the only patient in the hospital who was receiving that much education; she loved it, though. It made her feel "normal," like she was doing what she was supposed to be doing.

Ed and I needed to put a plan in place that would get us home as quickly as possible. I had to learn everything there was to know about taking care of Brooke. Everything. I had to know everything that the nurses knew, and do everything that the aides did. I had to know everything that the respiratory therapists knew, and do everything that the physical therapists did. I had to be all these people, and be able to do all their jobs. We needed to make extensive changes at home. We lived in a colonial-style house where all the bedrooms were on the second floor and all the doorways and halls were too narrow for a wheelchair. We needed ramps to get Brooke in and out of the house and a specialized bathroom that could accommodate her.

"We have a family decision to make, Brooke," I said. "We need to either sell our house and buy a one-story ranch or totally renovate what we have now. What do you think? How would you feel if we moved?"

"I don't want to move," Brooke said. "I don't think I could stand going to another strange place. I want to go home, Mom. I want to go home to our house," she said.

That made our decision much easier. We would renovate. While I was working on my part at the hospital, Ed was starting to put things in place at home. John, his close friend, Little League coaching partner, tea buddy from Stony Brook Hospital, fellow Eucharistic minister, and frequent visitor to rehab in New Jersey, was a carpenter. It was no surprise that they started this project together. They started making plans for the renovation in December and broke ground the first week in January 1991. The plan was to gut all the downstairs rooms to make them bigger and accessible, add a bedroom and accessible bathroom on the ground floor, and build a ramp on the side of the house and a deck on the back so Brooke could get in and out. It was a huge undertaking that was being started in the dead of winter. It was going to be difficult to do at that time of year, but the sooner we got started, the sooner we could get Brooke home.

The cost was going to be a problem. We were having enough trouble making ends meet before Brooke's accident, and it didn't look like I would be able to return to work anytime in the near future. The mailbox was also filling up with bills from the hospitals and from doctors, some of whom we had never even heard of. We had borrowed money and gotten help from family, but it wasn't enough to cover all the expenses.

"John, I'm not sure yet how I'm going to pay for this," Ed said.

"I know," John said. "Jackie and I, Pearl, and Vinnie from Little League have started a fund for you guys. We're calling it

The Friends of Brooke Ellison Fund, and I think it will help you out."

The whole community got involved. Vinnie ran a doo-wop concert at the high school to raise money. The church got involved; the schools got involved; the Habers, a family in the neighborhood, decorated their house during the holidays to raise money. There were cake sales, bottle collections, and other fund-raisers. Neighbors not only helped raise money but also helped work on the renovation. Harold, our next-door neighbor, an elderly man who used to watch the kids on occasion, came over every day to either hammer a nail or just to help clean up. Mary and Dennis, our neighbors from across the street whose daughter Suzie was Brooke's best friend, pitched in regularly. Neighbors would just stop in from time to time to ask if they could help. Ed and I were overwhelmed and so grateful. It was a beautiful testament to what could be accomplished when there was a shared motivation that was based on love.

BROOKE

"BROOKIE-LOVE, I brought the video," my father said as he entered my room.

"How far did you get last week?" I asked.

"We did a lot, I can't wait to show you," he said.

My father, with all the renovations going on at home, was afraid I would be upset by all the changes. So, from the very first step in the process, the very first day of breaking ground, my father videotaped everything that was done. He would bring the video with him every Saturday for me to watch so that I could see the progress. Watching the tapes was great for me. There was always a crew of neighbors, family, and friends that would be helping and they would always send their love on camera. Taping the renovations made things a lot easier for me. I saw my house the way it was, the changes being made to it, and it gave me a short visit with everyone I missed.

"You're staying the whole week this time, right, Chabadee?" I asked.

"You betcha, it's party time," he said.

Every four weeks or so, my father would come to rehab and stay a week with me. Some of the people he worked with at Social Security donated some of their own vacation time so that he could do this. Without that, it couldn't have happened. It gave my mother a very needed break. She was exhausted. It not only gave her an opportunity to go home and spend time with Kysten and Reed, but it also gave my grandmother, who was under siege with the renovations, a chance to go home as well. Because our kitchen was torn apart, she had been reduced to cooking on a hot plate with everyone eating on an ironing board that was set up in my parents' bedroom. It also gave my father the opportunity to learn how to take care of me as well. He would, in essence, take my mother's place at the hospital. He would stay all day, just like my mother did, and sleep at my uncle Richie's house at night. He would attend all my therapies and participate in all my care. I would love it when he would come to spend the week. In the evening he would read to me, we would play games, watch movies, and talk. We would talk about everything.

The evening shift was always much more relaxed than the day shift; there were no therapies. One of my favorite nurses worked the evening shift. Her name was Joy and she couldn't have had a more appropriate name. I would sometimes get visitors in the evening, which would be the highlight of the day. Richie and

Miriam, Lisa and Denise would come very often. My grandparents would also come as often as they could and would bring my favorite Italian food, like meatballs, eggplant parmigiana, and fried artichoke hearts.

My aunt Amy, who lived in Manhattan, would also come to the hospital and spend time with us. She would bring love and support. Her visits were very important to us. Sometimes she would bring Laura from New York City, an intuitive and hands-on healer. Laura would come every couple of weeks, with gifts of chocolates, lotions, music, and videos—anything she thought would excite my senses. Laura lived a very exciting life and knew a lot of famous people. I loved it when she told me about them and them about me. She was effervescent and enthusiastic about life. Laura would use her energy to try to heal me. She would place her hands over me and we would both concentrate as hard as we could. Although I never saw any physical changes, the loving attention and encouragement that both she and my aunt gave me were immeasurable.

Sometimes Michael, my father's best friend from his childhood, would come and visit. He was a professor of music and lived in San Francisco but traveled all over the world to study and lecture. Michael would tell the funniest and most fascinating stories about his travels. He was a joy to listen to and he was one of the many Michaels in my life.

My father and my visitors were my connection to the outside world. They kept me sane. Being trapped both in my body and in the hospital, I lived vicariously through them. When I listened to the stories Laura would tell, I was Laura. When Michael told me about the places he had traveled to, I traveled there with him. When my father and I talked about my hopes and my fears, I knew he listened.

"It's going to be all right, Brookie-Love," he'd say. "It's going to be all right."

ONE OF THE STEPS to getting Brooke home was removing the halo brace that she had been wearing since her days at Stony Brook. Brooke's doctor and therapists were getting more and more concerned about the status of her neck, particularly the spinal column at C-2, -3 and C-5, -6, where there clearly had been some damage. Her spinal column was shifting forward and the doctors feared that, once the halo brace was removed, she would not be able to stop her head from falling forward. To remove the halo brace, Brooke would have to have surgery to stabilize her neck. From what we were learning from the doctors, the surgery that she needed would be extensive and dangerous. She would have to have an orthopedic surgeon and a neurosurgeon work together. Her neck would be stabilized by the insertion of bone, metal wires, and rods into her spinal column. Brooke would have to be transferred to a regular hospital in Newark because the rehab hospital was not equipped to perform surgeries. We got word in January that the surgery would be scheduled in early February. We had a month to prepare. No amount of time would have been enough.

Brooke's stabilization surgery was set for February 6. She had to go through all of the regular pre-op testing that everyone goes through before an operation, but she also had to have an MRI of her cervical spine. This meant leaving the rehab hospital for a day and going to another facility to have the procedure.

The MRI machine looked like a time capsule. Brooke's head and body had to be slid into the long cylinder, but she was not permitted to have anything metallic on or around her. Her halo brace was MRI compatible, but her ventilator was not. No one had anticipated this problem, but the procedure had to be done so the surgeons could see what they were up against. In order to take Brooke off the ventilator, someone would have to breathe for her manually with an Ambu bag. An Ambu bag looks like a small football with a fitting on the end that gets attached to the tracheostomy site in her neck. Someone has to squeeze the bag in and out, almost like slowly pumping up a bicycle tire, to force air in and out of her lungs.

A seven-foot-long tube was cut and attached to the Ambu bag. The bag was then attached to Brooke. The nurse started manually resuscitating Brooke and the MRI session began. The machine banged and thumped and rattled while I stared at Brooke's chest to see if it was moving up and down. It was the only way we could tell if she was breathing. I was afraid to even blink my eyes and I wished that Ed were there with me. I stared at Brooke for over an hour, terrified. I thought about the time when Brooke was an infant and she was in an oxygen tent in the hospital with pneumonia. I remembered staring at her chest then, afraid that she would stop breathing. I couldn't imagine how Brooke was feeling with all that noise, not able to speak, lying flat on her back so totally helpless and so medically fragile.

I couldn't help seeing the irony in this whole situation. The Gulf War had just started and I was catching snippets of it on the television at the hospital. On one side of the world, people were being mutilated and killed by the thousands. In my little world, so much effort and attention were being given to keeping my little girl alive. I couldn't understand this and nothing seemed to make sense anymore. I wanted this all to end and thought it would take a miracle for Brooke to survive her operation.

I STARED AT THE MAPLE TREE outside my window. It was my friend. It greeted me each morning when I woke up and bid me good night when I went to sleep. It was steady and predictable and it was my calendar. Its leaves, which had changed to bright yellow and red, were gone. Its wintry branches now looked like glass fingers reaching out, trying to grab my hand. It was February 5 and I wondered whether I would ever see my friend again.

My mother rode with me in the ambulance to Newark, and as he had done in the past, my father followed close behind in the family car. He had taken the week off from work to be with us. The trip to Newark took only about twenty minutes, but when we arrived, it felt like we were worlds away. The hospital was old and very dingy-looking. It seemed impossible that I was going to spend at least a week there, that it was the place where I was going to have my operation. After we went through admitting, a nurse brought my parents and me to the intensive care unit, which, at this hospital, was just one big room, divided in half, with sixteen beds in it.

I had arrived on a stretcher but was placed in a bed immediately. Preparations began for the surgery, which was scheduled for the next day. They took blood, vital signs, and medical information to make sure that everything was a go. It was strange, but I hoped that they would find some rare blood disease so I wouldn't have to go through with the operation. The surgeons met with my parents and me to advise us on what we should expect.

"The surgery is scheduled for eight A.M. and will probably

take about six or seven hours," the neurosurgeon said. "If all goes well we will soon be able to remove the halo brace and she'll just have to wear a cervical collar for about a month."

The doctors pulled my parents over to the side and spoke to them. I was unable to hear what they were saying, but from the look on my mother's face, I was glad I couldn't hear. The morning of the surgery came much more quickly than I wanted it to. My parents came into the unit early in the morning and saw me getting prepared for surgery. I was taken down to the operating room and my parents could only come as far as the waiting room.

"Please don't let them take me in there! Please make them stop. Don't make me go!" I screamed to my parents as I was wheeled down the hall to the operating room. I was certain I would never see them again.

When I opened my eyes I didn't believe that I was alive. The surgery had taken eight hours and I had survived. Everything was bleary and confusing from the anesthesia, but I realized that I had a bandage wrapped around my head and the halo brace had been removed.

"You look beautiful," my father said. "No more bars in front of your face."

Being paralyzed and in a halo brace is like being in a cage within a cage. The outer cage was now removed and I could be touched and I could be hugged. I still couldn't move, and I still couldn't breathe on my own, but I was alive.

A week after the surgery, I returned to rehab and I was so happy to be there. I was back where things were familiar and I was around people I knew cared. I saw my nurses, my teachers, and my therapists. I saw Keisha, Donna, and Lara, and as I was lifted back into bed I saw my friend the maple, still standing by the window waiting for my return.

IT WAS GETTING TO BE SPRINGTIME. I could feel it and smell it in the air. The daffodils had bloomed and the forsythia had made way for the azaleas and rhododendrons. Nature's reawakening only made us more keenly aware of our own rebirth. Discharge from rehab was imminent. The renovations at home were nearly complete, Brooke's wheelchair was being made, and Ed and I had passed the required tests to show that we could take care of Brooke. Being judged in our competency and fitness as Brooke's caregivers was a process I found most difficult to accept. Even with us having been deemed worthy, Brooke was still not allowed to come home until we had gotten a home nursing agency in place, a respiratory company lined up, and a medical supply house on board. Ed was handling most of those details and trying to resolve how all this was going to be paid for.

"Brooke, we're getting real close to going home," I said.

"Do you really think it's actually going to happen soon?"

"Oh, it will be soon, I just don't know exactly when," I said. "But it's going to be a lot sooner than everyone around here originally thought."

By the end of April, the renovation at home had been completed, we had a respiratory company and medical supply house, and we had gotten a nursing agency that said it could provide us with nurses. Because Brooke was on a ventilator, she needed nursing coverage twenty-four hours a day, seven days a week.

"I think we're just about all set down here to get you guys home," Ed said to me on the phone early in May.

"I can't believe it, honey, that's great," I said. "Were you able to resolve the insurance issues?" I asked. "How are we going to pay for everything?"

"It looks like our insurance company will pay for some of the medical expenses and state Medicaid will pay for some of the nursing. I'm also fighting for some nursing hours from our insurance company. Until then, we are going to have to take care of Brooke the remaining hours of the day."

"We will still be able to take Brooke home, won't we?" I asked.

"As long as we have an agency to provide nurses and the hospital can turn Brooke over to a nurse when she gets here, we'll be okay, but I'm still working on trying to get full nursing coverage. We are going to have to do this to get Brooke home," Ed said.

Finally, a discharge date was set: May 16. It was almost too hard to believe that it was actually going to happen; it really seemed too good to be true. That weekend when Ed and Reed came to visit, most of the time was spent packing up and cleaning out Brooke's area of the room. All of her pictures and posters were taken down, her stuffed animals and trinkets were put into boxes, and all her clothes except for just enough to get her through the next few days were sent home. Keisha, Donna, and some of Brooke's other friends also came to help and watch. We were happy to be going home but sad to be leaving the other girls behind. It was like the last day of school when everything is being packed up for the summer and you know you're not going to see some of your friends until September. This time, though, we knew it was likely that we would never see these girls again.

Tuesday night, the night before Brooke's discharge, Richie and Miriam had come up for one last visit. We were sitting, and talking, at Brooke's bedside.

"Jean," one of the nurses called into the room. "Your husband's on the phone."

"That's strange," I said to Richie. "I was supposed to call him." I went to the nurses' station and took the call.

"What's up, honey?" I asked, excited about going home.

"Brooke can't come home tomorrow," Ed said.

"What? You're kidding, right?"

"No, I wish I were. The nursing agency can't staff the case yet."

"Why not? I thought everything was worked out," I said.

"They can't get any nurses," Ed said.

"Not even one nurse to meet us at the door," I said in disbelief.

"Not even one nurse. It's either because there're none available or there's some problem with how much they're going to get paid. All I know is, I'm not getting a straight answer from anybody."

"What am I going to tell Brooke?" I said. "How can I tell her she's not going home tomorrow? Everything's already packed. They even had a going-away party for her. I can't believe this. What's it going to take, a miracle to get out of here?"

"I'm working on it," Ed said. "Give me a day or two. I'll let you know as soon as I know something."

Maybe some of the people around here were right, I thought. Maybe Brooke would never be discharged. So many things had to be put in place, and so many details had to be worked out. Even if we did everything we were supposed to do, it seemed that there were still so many things that were beyond our control. If the nursing agency couldn't provide just one nurse on the very first day, what did that tell us about the future? I thought. How were we going to get Brooke home, and how were we going to manage when we got there? I was upset and frustrated, and I had to go back into the room and tell Brooke.

PART TWO

In the depths of winter I finally learned
there was in me an invincible summer.

—ALBERT CAMUS

"I'M RIGHT HERE, hold my hand, and don't be frightened," my mother would say to me when I was little. "And don't worry, that's my job. That's what mothers are for," she'd say.

Her hand lay on top of mine, our fingers woven together as tightly as our two lives had been over the past eight months. I scanned the snapshots in my mind to find a picture, a mental photograph that would help me remember how it used to feel. The calming movement of her thumb against my fingers, her skin so soft and warm and my hand lost in hers. My brain was physically separated from my body, but my mind needed to remain connected to my soul. I had to remember. I couldn't lose those images.

I stared closely at our hands; my mother's wedding band was the only distinction between them. I couldn't tell where her fingers started and mine ended. Our hands were one. My mother was sitting to the right of my bed, as she usually did. She fed me, talked to me, and read to me from my right side. When she sleeps with my father, she sleeps on the right side of the bed, too. It had been eight months since my parents had slept together in their own bed, but that was about to change. I was going home.

It had only been five days since my mother had given me the news about our not being able to go home. She was so upset and so worried about me. I was upset and worried about her. We were both upset and worried about my father. He was frustrated and angry and felt responsible for a situation he couldn't control. He was upset and worried about us. He had gotten the situation tentatively resolved and some nursing had been put in place. We were set to leave, ready to go home, and somehow it all seemed impossible to believe.

"Do you really think it's going to happen this time, Mom?" I asked.

"It's going to happen," she said, looking out into the hallway. "It's going to happen sooner than you think."

The ambulance crew that was to take us home had arrived.

"We've seen a few of these, haven't we, Mom?" I said.

"Yes, we have, but if it hadn't been for the Setauket rescue squad at the accident or for the Stony Brook fire chief who was driving in the car behind the one that hit you, you wouldn't be here right now," she said. "That fire chief started CPR within minutes and he saved your life. It was a miracle that he was there."

"Do you know who he was?" I asked.

"I never found out his name," my mother said.

I thought about all the people who had come into my life. The people without whom I never would have survived. There were so many. Were they just doing their jobs or was it just a coincidence that our paths had crossed? That was hard for me to believe, it had to be much more than that.

I looked around the room, knowing that it would be the

last time I would ever see it. Keisha, Donna, and Lara were all at their therapies. We had said our good-byes. We had all cried and said that we would keep in touch and see each other again, but I knew how difficult that was going to be. I took in everything and held a mental picture in my mind: the mechanical beds, the bed tables stocked with medications, creams, and lotions; the fluorescent light fixtures on the walls behind each bed that were so typically hospital. I had been in that room for eight months and wondered if it was a picture I really wanted to keep in my mental scrapbook.

As difficult and as painful as my life in the hospital had been, it was a time I had shared with my mother. A bond had been forged between us that was unique. I had received from her true love, unconditional love, the kind of love that is given from a mother to an infant. She bathed me, brushed my teeth, combed my hair. She got me dressed in the morning and undressed at night. She was my arms and my legs. I was her daughter, and with that came all the hopes and dreams that she had for me. And although our lives weren't turning out the way we had expected, she was determined to make it work. We were going home, we were going to resume our lives, we were going to try to make some sense out of all of this. She had worked so hard, done her best, and I knew I had to do all I could to make it worth it.

"Thank you, Mom," I said.

"For what," she said.

"For, you know, everything."

"Oh, don't thank me, that's what mothers are for," she said. "I love you."

"I love you, too, Mom. I love you, too."

"DID YOU CLICK YOUR HEELS three times when I wasn't looking, Mom?" Brooke said, gazing out the rear window of the ambulance. "We're actually going home."

"I've been clicking my heels for about a week now," I said. "I think this morning it actually worked."

It was hard for me to accept the idea that we were traveling in an ambulance to a destination I was not dreading. The nervous anticipation I was feeling was not fear but happy excitement.

"Do you think there will be anyone at home to meet us besides Dad, Kysten, Reed, and Grandma?" Brooke asked.

"I don't know what to expect," I said. "We'll see when we get there."

I really didn't know how anything was going to work out when we got home. I knew that nursing was going to be a problem and that I would still have to be involved in Brooke's care. Kysten and Reed had been without me for so long and I wanted to spend more time with them. Kysten, in particular, was having trouble adjusting and accepting what had happened, and I knew she was going to need more of my time. I wanted to return to work, not only because we needed the money but because it was something I had worked so hard to prepare for. I wanted to be a teacher, but I also knew I was going to have to be a nurse. I still needed to be a wife and a mother. I didn't know how I was going to balance all of these things.

I reached into my pocket and pulled out a little card that Ed had given me in rehab. It had the "serenity prayer" written on it.

It was a prayer that I had heard many times in the past but had never really listened to:

God grant me the Serenity to accept the things I cannot change. Courage to change the things I can. And Wisdom to know the difference.

In rehab, I said that prayer over and over to myself each day. I was having a lot of difficulty with the first and third parts. I was trying to learn a life's lesson, but doing it the hard way. Before Brooke's accident, it seemed that everything was going along the way I had planned. There were minor bumps but no real major unanticipated results. From the day of her accident, however, nothing turned out the way I had thought. Other than my belief that we would be all right, each step along the way to realizing that goal was different from what I had anticipated. I had come to realize that I couldn't really plan or control anything, but I also felt that I couldn't completely abdicate either. I had to know what I could do, while also realizing what was out of my hands.

"We're getting close, Brooke," I said as the ambulance drove down Nesconset Highway passed the Smith Haven Mall. I loved to go shopping there with the girls and I wondered whether we would be able to do that again. As we drove down Nicolls Road and turned into our development, everything seemed different. Nothing had really physically changed, but it was as if I were seeing things for the first time. As we pulled down Sycamore Drive, I saw the park on the right where the kids played Little League baseball. There were kids throwing a ball around and I realized that the season was probably in full swing by now. I remembered how the constant ringing of the phone during the season used to bother me; now I wished I had been home to hear it this past year. As we turned the corner onto our street, I felt my heart racing and pounding in my chest. I didn't know whether to laugh or cry or just scream out. The ambulance pulled up in front of the house and began to back in.

"We're here, sweetheart. I can't believe it, but we're really here," I said.

Brooke was lying on the stretcher, her head tilted up enough for her to see out the back window. She could see the basketball hoop that Ed and our neighbor Dennis had put up for the kids to use. Under it was a throng of people who had gathered for her arrival. I smiled at her and she smiled back.

"There's no place like home, Mom," she said. "There's no place like home."

BROOKE

THE BALLOONS THAT HAD BEEN TIED to the mailbox had been taken down. The big pastel-colored signs hanging over the door that read WELCOME HOME BROOKE and WE MISSED YOU had been removed. It was the evening and everyone except my family and the nurse that had been assigned to me had gone.

"It's been a pretty amazing day, hasn't it, Brookie-Love," my father said.

"Amazing," I said, almost too tired to fully comprehend what had happened during the day.

The community had rallied. My family and neighbors, my friends from school, and my friends from karate had all come to greet me when I got home. It was overwhelming. Most of the people who were there were people I hadn't seen since before my accident. Mixed with the excitement of seeing them was the apprehension of how they would react when they saw me. This was the first time they would be seeing the new me. I was different on the outside, really different, but only on the outside. On the inside, I was the same person I had always been. I wasn't sure, though, whether everybody would understand that. I was especially concerned about my friends. I didn't want what had happened to me to change our relationship. Now that I was home, I needed them more than ever. I needed something "normal" to hold on to.

"It was good to see everyone from the karate school, wasn't it, Brooke," my mother said.

"It was great," I said, "but Sensei Joyce said that Kysten and Reed haven't been back to class since my accident. Did you know that, Mom?" I said.

"Yes," she said. "I didn't tell you, though."

"Reed!" I called my brother over from the couch where he was sitting. "You have to promise me that you will go back to karate. Both you and Kysten have to promise me," I said.

"I don't want to go back if you can't," Reed said.

"You have to go back," I said. "You have to finish what we started. Remember what Dad always says: It's not what you start that counts, it's what you finish. You have to do this, if not for yourself, then do it for me."

I knew that the repercussions of my accident had affected everyone in the family. Our lives had been turned upside down and inside out. The thought of Kysten and Reed not finishing karate and not getting their black belts because of me was something I could not accept. This was something I could control. They were going back.

My mother and father lifted me out of the wheelchair that

the ambulance crew had put me in when I arrived home. I was going back to bed in my room, in my house. It was a new bed, a hospital-style bed, one that moved up and down and had side rails. It wasn't my old bed, but it was mine. I had moved into a new room, one that had been built for me on the first floor and had its own bathroom. It wasn't my old room, but it was mine.

My father sat with me while my mother went upstairs to take a shower.

"What do you think, Dad?" I said. "Did you get the feeling that my friends were uncomfortable around me?"

"Oh no," he said. "You have to remember that we've been living with this for eight or nine months now. You're going to have to give everybody else a chance to get adjusted. You can't expect everything to snap right back to the way it used to be," he said. "Give it some time, Brookie-Love. Don't worry, just give it some time."

I really didn't want to give it time. Now that I was home, I wanted things to be how they used to be. All through my time in the hospital I had held on to my memories of how things were. I was home, but things were different. My mother came into my room. She was wearing a bathrobe and her hair was all wrapped up in a towel, just like it always was after a shower. It was familiar, so beautifully familiar. She looked at me and at my father and then she looked around the room.

"Where's my clip?" she said, perplexed. "Have either of you seen my clip?"

I looked back at her, smiled, and sighed. This was a good start, I thought, this was a very good start.

IN HIGH SCHOOL, some of my friends tried to get me to join the Future Nurses of America, a club organized for girls who wanted to become nurses. I never could understand the whole candy-striper craze. Being a nurse was the last job on my list of possible career choices. Needless to say, I didn't join. Back then, I really didn't know what I wanted to do, or what direction my life was going to go in. What I did know, however, was that bedpans and blood pressure cuffs were not going to be the tools of the trade I ultimately chose. It wasn't that I thought nursing was beneath me or that I had some grandiose ideas about where my life was going—quite the contrary. I just couldn't do it. I was too squeamish. It was something about me, a facet of my personality of which I was not particularly proud. A weakness in me, I thought, one I would never readily admit to. The girls I knew who chose to be nurses had my utmost respect and admiration. They were dedicating their lives to the care of others. What more noble a job could there be?

I knew that when we got home we were going to have to make adjustments and changes to the way we were used to living. I just didn't know how huge those adjustments and changes were going to have to be. In rehab, I learned how to take care of Brooke, but I thought that I would be the backup in case of an emergency. I thought the nurses who came to the house, like the nurses in rehab, would be the primary caregivers. I couldn't have been more wrong. The nursing agency we were first involved with sent nurses to the house when they were able to secure them. And that was not often. We would get a knock at the door at eleven in the evening and it would be a nurse ready to report for the eleven-to-seven overnight shift. It would be someone we had never met or who had never met Brooke. Either Ed or I would have to explain what was required for Brooke's care while the other one tried to get some rest. Sometimes a nurse would stay a night or two and sometimes she would last as long as a week. Ultimately, however, she would move on. Another one would report, we would train her, and she would move on, too. Nursing care was sporadic and the difference in the levels of competence was dramatic.

One nurse who had reported for an overnight shift introduced herself to Brooke, picked up her Ambu bag, and said, "So this is your ventilator." Another didn't know the difference between a suction catheter and a urethral catheter. One had arrived after having taken too much of her own "medication," and one came to the house with her children. Some wanted us to pick them up before work and others wanted to be driven back home afterward.

On the one hand, we had this litany of nightmares, while on the other, we had nurses who were professional, dedicated, and loving. Many stayed for a while, developed a rapport with Brooke and the family, but eventually had to move on as well. Some were young and were starting families. Others left for better jobs in hospitals and elsewhere, because most of the nursing agencies didn't pay as well or provide benefits.

One evening in May, a couple of days after we had gotten home, a new nurse reported for the three-to-eleven evening shift. Her name was Debby. She was about thirty-four years old and was married to a New York City police officer. It was a nasty night with heavy rain, thunder, and lightning. With the experience that we had with nurses, we really didn't expect her to show up. Not long after she arrived, we lost electrical power, our house was hit by lightning, and we smelled smoke. The fire department, knowing the address, sent two fire trucks and an ambulance to the house. About a dozen firemen came in with hoses and axes ready to break into the newly renovated walls. Fortunately they found the problem before any damage was done.

"This isn't a typical day in the Ellison house," I said to Debby, wondering what she must have been thinking.

"You must think we're the Murphys from 'Murphy's Law,' " Ed said.

"Do you think you'll want to take a chance and come back again?" I said.

"I think so," Debby said, undaunted. "This wasn't so bad."

She not only came back the following day, but she has been with us ever since.

Debby was the exception, the only nurse we could count on to be there when we needed her.

It became very clear to me early on, after we got home, that the majority of the nursing responsibilities were going to fall on me. I couldn't count on the nurses coming when they were supposed to, and when they did come, how dedicated they were going to be to the job. Taking care of Brooke was a twenty-four-hour-a-day job. This was not what I wanted, nor was it what I expected. I needed to be able to spend time with Kysten and Reed. Ed and I wanted to be able to have some time alone. I wanted to start my teaching career. I wanted to be Brooke's mother, not her nurse.

Life is full of ironies. I think it was Woody Allen who said, "If you want to make God laugh, tell him about your future plans." As it was turning out, the one job that I said I would never do, I was doing. Maybe my friends in high school knew something I didn't know back then. I was going to become a member of their club whether I wanted to or not. It was just going to take me twenty years longer to join.

BEING HOME AND NOT GETTING UP and going to school each day was peculiar. It didn't feel right. Kysten and Reed would get up, have breakfast, get dressed, run into my room and say good-bye. My routine would just be getting under way. What took Kysten and Reed about a half hour in the morning, took my mother and me anywhere between three and four hours to do. Doing my medical care, taking care of my personal needs, getting me dressed, up into my chair and fed was a long, difficult, and tedious process. My mother never complained and I tried not to as well. There were some times, though, that were harder than others.

Every year in June, as the school year drew to a close, we would have our dance recital. It was a big event that usually spanned three nights and was held at a local university. It was a time that Kysten and I looked forward to and it would come after we had worked all year on various routines in tap, jazz, and ballet. It was a big occasion for the whole family. My parents would always buy us flowers, and even though it would invariably fall on Reed's birthday, he would love to get his picture taken with us all dressed up in our costumes. June 1991 was the first year since Kysten's first recital ten years earlier that there would be no dancing. It was almost more than I could bear. I had come to grips with my situation, but every now and again there would be a reminder. A glimpse at the past that I wanted back but knew I couldn't have. Some things really seemed unfair, and not being able to dance was one of the worst.

Missing that recital was a slap in the face, a kick in the behind, a glaring example of what I was unable to do. If I dwelled on that, I knew I would be finished. I could stay in bed all day and watch TV, and probably everybody except my parents would say they wouldn't blame me. I couldn't do that to my parents and I couldn't do that to myself. I had to focus on what I was still able to do. I could still think, and I could still learn. I had to get back to school.

Even though I had gotten schooling twice a day every day while I was in the hospital, it wasn't going to be enough for me to resume with my class that next September. My mother was still very much aware of the promise she had made to me when I was in ICU in Stony Brook Hospital, and she was going to do everything in her power to make good on that promise. Plans were put in place for me to get home schooling every day over the summer. Each day, Monday through Friday, was to be dedicated to a certain subject. I was going to get three hours a day of one-on-one teaching and no subject was going to be spared; I was going to get home taught in seventh grade honors English, social studies, math, science, and Latin. This was with the expectation that, by September, I would have completed the seventh grade curriculum and would be prepared to start the eighth grade with my class.

I had four teachers that taught at the junior high: Dr. Brooks for science, Ms. Driscoll for math, Mr. Betcher for English and social studies, and Mr. Gravino for Latin. I was a little nervous at first because I was going to be alone with each one of them. I didn't know how they were going to react to me or if they would feel uncomfortable with my situation. I also felt that I had something to prove, not so much to them but to myself. I needed to show that I could still do well and I didn't want anybody cutting me any slack or feeling sorry for me because of what had happened to me. Any nervousness that I may have had at the start of the summer was eliminated very quickly because of the wonderful teachers these people were. Both Ms. Driscoll and Dr. Brooks were serious enough to teach me what I needed to know but kind and relaxed enough to make me feel very comfortable in "class." Mr. Betcher, whose specialty was history, was in his mid-fifties, was the school's lacrosse coach, a summer camp counselor, and a driver's education instructor at the high school. All the kids loved him and anyone who got one of his classes was considered lucky. His reputation was well deserved.

"Tonight, Brooke, we're going to study Dolly Madison," he'd say.

"I don't mean the first lady, I mean the ice cream." He'd whip out a pint of ice cream, make sundaes, and tell historical anecdotes that would enliven his history lesson.

My studies in Latin were a unique experience. I had never taken a foreign language before, and even though I had gotten some tutoring in Latin when I was in the hospital, this was going to be my first time studying it on an official basis. Mr. Gravino was the only Latin teacher in the junior high school and I didn't know very much about him. I was supposed to have him in the seventh grade. When I was in the hospital, he had made audio-cassettes for me with word pronunciations, verb conjugations, and noun declensions. From his voice on the cassettes, he sounded a little bit dry and stoic. When he arrived the first day on his motorcycle, I realized I couldn't have been more wrong.

Mr. Gravino was a short man, about five feet five inches tall, round in the middle, and bald on top. When he arrived that first day he was wearing a black T-shirt that said on the pocket

"Hades Manes," which I later found out was the Latin translation of Hell's Angels. I didn't know what to make of him.

At first I got the sense, not from anything he said but rather from his attitude, that Mr. Gravino thought I wouldn't be able to keep up in Latin and should probably be taking a language that would not be as demanding. I got the feeling that he thought that he was wasting his time, that I wouldn't last very long, and that ultimately I wouldn't be in his class in September. He wasn't easy on me, which is what I wanted, and I proved not only to myself but also to him that he was wrong. We became great friends. By the end of the summer I had fulfilled my requirements and was ready to go back to school. The thought of getting up in the morning, going off to school and not having Kysten and Reed leave me behind was almost unimaginable, but it looked like that dream just might come true. The dreams I had about dancing, though, came at night. They were wonderful, vivid, and exhilarating dreams. I moved with ease to the music, feeling every jump, every spin, and every move. They were so real. Not all of our dreams turn out the way we expect them to. Sometimes we wake up and find that life is different from what we had planned. I can't move my body but I can still dance. I dance in my mind, I dance in my heart, and I dance effortlessly in my dreams when I go to sleep at night.

JEAN

AS THE SUMMER MOVED ALONG, both Brooke and I were getting anxious about getting back to school. She wanted to go back to learn, I wanted to go back to teach. With the amount of time

I needed to devote to Brooke's care, I wasn't sure whether I was going to be able to return to work. Watching Brooke interact with the teachers that came to the house over the summer, however, made it even more clear to me that I had to honor the promise I had made to her that she would be able to go back to school. She enjoyed the academic challenge, the exchange of ideas, and I think most important, the social interaction. She was happiest when she was around people.

While Brooke was catching up on her studies, Ed and I made plans to meet with the committee for special education, the CSE, to set up Brooke's individual education plan. The CSE was a team of people associated with the school district that met to assess the needs of students with special circumstances. Each member of the committee would vote on the specific recommendations of the district and the individual requests made by the parents. We met early in the summer to give us enough time to resolve any possible problems that might occur with Brooke's plan. Her plan was unique. Never before in our district had a student on life support attended a class in the mainstream. Having been trained in special education, I knew what Brooke's rights were and what the school district was required to provide for her.

When I requested Brooke's textbooks and assignments in her first weeks at rehab, I made our intentions clear to the school district. I told them at that time that Brooke planned to return to school and that she wanted to be with her class. The director of special education and her assistant visited with us while we were still in rehab and they seemed very open to the idea. Both Ed and I were very thankful and pleased that we weren't meeting any resistance. There were the obvious concerns that needed to be addressed in order for Brooke to return to school. A specially equipped bus would have to be provided to transport her. There would have to be someone to take notes for Brooke, since she wasn't able to write for herself. And most important, she would need a nurse to monitor her ventilator and take care of any personal needs that she would have during the day.

When we met with the CSE, we were able to agree on all of the items set forth in Brooke's educational plan except the nursing issue. The district felt that nursing was not an educational responsibility but rather a medical expense, which was our responsibility to provide. We believed, on the other hand, that since it was the school district's responsibility to educate Brooke in the least restrictive environment, and since she could not go to school without a nurse, it was their responsibility to supply one. The fact of the matter was, even if we had agreed to provide the nurse for Brooke, there was no one available or reliable enough to come five days a week during the school year to cover that shift. In effect, if Brooke had to rely on nurses that were being provided by the nursing agency, she would not have gotten back to school. The district couldn't take Brooke back without a nurse and they wouldn't provide one. We couldn't provide one either, so we were stuck.

The CSE agreed to take the nursing issue before the school board for a vote. If the school board voted yes, the CSE would go along with their decision. The school board voted, and all but one member voted against us. No one wanted to take responsibility for approving nursing. It had never been done before and no one wanted to set a precedent. After the vote was announced, Ed called all of the board members personally to try to get an understanding of the rationale behind their decision.

For some of the board members it was a matter of money: the expense would be too great. Others felt that Brooke didn't belong in a mainstream setting and should either be sent to a special school for disabled children or tutored at home with the teachers from the junior high school. Both Ed and I felt that sending Brooke out of the community or tutoring her at home was not the answer. Brooke needed to get back out there. She needed to move on, get out of the house and into the community and not be shut away from the rest of society. We also felt that no matter where she went to school, she would still need a nurse and it would be just as costly. This logic made no sense to either one of us.

Ed asked the president of the school board if he could make one last presentation to them at their next meeting. It was the last meeting before the new school year was to start. Ed went armed with the regulations in special education law, points about the cost effectiveness of nursing vis-à-vis home tutoring, and with the hope that they would appreciate our dilemma. It was something that Ed didn't want to do, but was something he felt he had to try in order to get Brooke back to school. The board listened, took another vote, and denied the request again.

With just a day to go before school started on September 4, we didn't know what was going to happen. We tried to secure a nurse on our own, but that didn't work out and the district was not budging on this issue.

"We have to make this work," I said. "I can't allow school to start and not have Brooke be there. I promised her."

We were running out of time and running out of options.

"What if I go to school with Brooke?" I said to Ed. "I can take care of Brooke as well as any nurse can." It was the only thing I could think of that might work.

"I don't know if the district will go for it," Ed said. "It certainly won't cost them anything. If you're willing to go and Brooke's okay with it, then let's see if the district will allow it."

I called the superintendent's office and they agreed. They would allow me to attend class with Brooke provided I had a doctor certify that I was able to care for her. On September 3, the day before school started and the day before the anniversary of her accident, we were set to go.

Instead of my standing in front of the class as the teacher, I would be sitting in the back as a nurse. The important thing, though, was that Brooke would be sitting in class as a student. We were both going back to school, and although it wasn't what we had originally planned, I had kept my promise.

B R O O K E

"HOW DO I LOOK?" I said to my father when he came back into my room after he got dressed for work.

"You're the most beautiful girl I've ever seen," he said. "Except for maybe the first time I laid eyes on your mother."

"No I'm not."

"You most definitely are and no one can tell me anything different," he said.

"No I'm not," I said again.

My father was always saying things like that to me. He would always tell me how good I looked and then I would always negate it. He'd put up a fuss and I'd tell him to stop. I knew that he was trying to build me up, and even though I liked when he did it, I felt that I knew better. I wasn't feeling all that great about how I looked and I was nervous about going back to school.

It was September 4, 1991, exactly one year from the day of my accident, and again it was the first day of school. I couldn't believe that a year had passed, and because it was the anniversary of my accident, I couldn't stop myself from thinking about that day and what had happened to me since then. No one in the house had really talked about "the anniversary." It may have been that so much attention and effort had been put into trying to get things settled and me back into school that there wasn't time to dwell on that. It also may have been a conscious effort on everyone's part to avoid it. In either case, no one had said anything about this being "the day." It was peculiar, though, with all the excitement and hustle to get me ready, I could sense a sadness in both my mother and father. Behind their obvious attempts to keep me upbeat and distracted, I knew there was the nagging memory of what had happened just a year ago. I caught my father and mother looking at each other, not saying anything, but their watery-eyed message was clear. They were speaking to each other without saying a word. They didn't want me to know what they were feeling.

"What time is the minibus coming?" I asked, trying to distract them from what they were thinking.

"I don't know," my father said. "I'll check the schedule on the refrigerator." He bolted out of the room, needing an excuse to wipe his eyes and blow his nose.

"Seven-thirty," my mother whispered. "You knew that. Were you just checking to see if we knew?"

I was getting such a strange sense of déjà vu. I couldn't tell if this was something that had actually happened before or whether it was just something reminiscent of what had gone on a year ago. So much of what was going on seemed familiar, but this year was so much different. Like last year, I was concerned about my appearance and whether I would fit in. Unlike last year, though, I was concerned about my wheelchair, not my outfit, and not just about whether I would fit in but whether both my mother and I would be accepted. I wondered how everyone was going to react to me and to her. This had never been done before. No one had ever gone to school like this with their mother. I was confused and didn't know what emotion to feel.

My father stayed in my room with me while my mother went upstairs to shower and get dressed. That was how it worked. They both would get me ready in the morning. My mother would get me dressed in bed and then my father would help lift me into my wheelchair. Once I was in my chair, my father would get Kysten and Reed up and get ready for work. When he came down, my mother would go and get ready herself. We had developed a routine over the summer, and everything was done the way my mother liked it, by the numbers. Someone had to be nearby all the time because of my ventilator. If I became disconnected from the ventilator, someone had to be there to troubleshoot the problem and fix it.

"Brookie-Love, I just want you to get through the day," my father said. "No more than that. Look at how far you've come from this time last year. You have nothing to prove."

It was the only reference my father made to my accident and that he knew what I was thinking and feeling. I felt, however, that I did have something to prove, not only to myself but also to the school board. I needed to prove that I could succeed. I wanted them to know that they were making a mistake by not helping me and my family. I knew my mother and father didn't want me to feel any more pressure than I was already experiencing. Making the adjustments to the huge physical and psychological changes in my life were enough to deal with.

"Just get through the day," my father said again. "And don't worry, that's my job. Remember the old saying: Yesterday is history / Tomorrow is a mystery / Today is a gift / That's why they call it the present."

"I know, Dad, thanks, but I don't want you to worry either. I'll be all right."

Everything was different but so much seemed the same. Instead of holding hands and walking to the bus stop with my father, I was in my wheelchair and waiting for the minibus with my mother. The divergent paths that my mother and I had set out on only a year ago had merged. It was as if something wasn't allowing us to set out individually on our own.

I heard my mother's high heels clicking across the ceramic tiles outside my bedroom.

"What did you say?" my mother asked when she came into the room.

"Oh, nothing, Dad and I were just talking," I said.

"How do I look?" my mother said, standing in the doorway.

She was wearing a blue print dress with matching heels and the sun was reflecting off her long brown hair. My father looked at her and then at me and paused.

"I am the luckiest man on the planet," he said.

We all smiled, and before my mother could say anything, I said, "It's on my bathroom sink."

"Thanks, honey," she said as she grabbed her hair clip and snapped it in place.

"Let's go get 'em," she said as if we were about to go to war.

"I'm ready," I said, but I knew full well that neither one of us had any idea what to expect.

"DO YOU THINK the bus is lost or do you think they forgot about us?" I asked Ed while we were standing in the driveway waiting for the minibus to arrive.

"I don't know, but if it's not here in a couple of minutes, I'll drive you," he said.

Just the night before, we had gotten our new van. We had pushed the dealer to get it delivered before school started just in case there was a problem with the school's transportation. We still hadn't tried it out yet. We hadn't gone visiting or shopping, to a movie or a restaurant since Brooke had gotten home. As a matter of fact, it was not only Brooke's first day back at school but it was her first time venturing out past her own backyard in a year. The bus pulled up at about 7:45.

"Let's get this show on the road," I said.

"Wait, let me get Reed, I have to take some pictures," Ed said. "It wouldn't be the first day of school without some pictures."

Reed, who was in the middle of finishing up his cornflakes, came out for a couple of shots and to say good-bye. His bus came a little later and it felt strange that we were saying good-bye to him. This was the first year that all three kids were in separate schools. Kysten, who had left earlier, was in tenth grade and it was her first day at Ward Melville High School. Reed was in the sixth grade and it was his last year at Nassakeag Elementary School, and it was Brooke's first day in the eighth grade at Murphy Junior High.

We were all nervous, but none of us wanted to let on just how nervous we were. It was a short trip to the junior high. We just had to wind our way out of the development, cross over Nicolls

Road, and we were there. Ed, after leaving Reed in the hands of our neighbor Harold, followed behind the bus in our car. He wanted to see that we got there all right and to make sure that there were no problems when we arrived at school.

Since the bus had arrived late at the house, we arrived late to school. All of the buses had left the bus circle and no one was outside except two school board members who were standing at the door. They were either keeping vigil or waiting for us. Ed helped Brooke and me out of the van and helped carry my bags. I had my big black pocketbook; a book bag with notebooks, pens, pencils, and other school supplies; and a large blue duffel bag with Brooke's medical supplies. It must have looked like we had packed up our house and were ready to move in.

"What the heck are they doing here?" Ed whispered, referring to the school board members.

"Maybe they're the welcoming committee," I said.

"If they're the welcoming committee, then my name is General Custer and this must be Little Big Horn," Ed said.

We both tried not to laugh as we made our way to the front door. Ed nodded his head to the school board members and they nodded back to us. Nothing was said, not a word. I knew that Brooke was frightened to see them, but by the looks on their faces they seemed more frightened to see us. We passed by like a military review and I wondered whether we had passed their inspection. They had never seen Brooke, and I don't think they knew what to expect. It was too late, though. Brooke was there and I was there and nothing was going to stop us from going through those front doors.

I held the door and Ed pushed Brooke over the bump in the doorway.

"We're in," I said. "We made it."

"It's hard to believe, but I'm back," Brooke said with a nervous smile.

"Remember what I said, Brookie-Love, just get through the day," Ed said. "Both of you, just get through the day. No matter what happens, I'm so proud of you."

Ed kissed Brooke on the forehead and me on the cheek. Then he whispered in my ear, "I love you guys, kick ass and take names," he said.

The second part was an expression he always used when he wanted one of us to be tough. He winked at me, I smiled back at him, and I turned and went down the hallway with Brooke. The next phase of our journey had begun.

BROOKE

IN STARK CONTRAST to the "greeting" we received from the school board members, my mother and I were met by Ms. Calligheris, my special education coordinator. She came running down the hall when she saw us and was genuinely excited and happy to see us. She was tall with blond hair, in her twenties, and a bundle of frenetic energy. She had so many plans and ideas about what we were going to do that when she spoke, her mouth couldn't keep up with her brain.

"Hello, Brooke, hello, Mrs. Ellison, I'm so happy to meet you," she said without taking a breath. "I've heard so much about you. This is going to be great, this is going to be really great. I can't wait to get started. You've got great classes and great teachers, and they're all anxious to meet you, too. Oh, but you know some of them already, don't you? You have Dr. Brooks for earth science and Mr. Gravino for Latin and Mr. Betcher for social studies. You know all of them from the summer, right? You have Mr. Lyons for English and Mrs. Dunton for math. You're going to like them, too. We're going to do neat things this year and you're going to do great. You, too, Mrs. Ellison, you're going to do great, too. Oh, gee, I'm running off at the mouth here, and I didn't even introduce you to your tutors."

Standing patiently behind Ms. Calligheris were two women about my mother's age who were assigned to take notes for me during the school day.

"This is Mrs. Schlitz and Mrs. Graham," Ms. Calligheris said, a little embarrassed for not having introduced them right away. Mrs. Schlitz, who was short and had short blond hair, had my morning classes, and Mrs. Graham, who was tall with long brown hair, had my afternoon classes.

"Mrs. Schlitz and I were looking over your course materials," Mrs. Graham said. "You've got some pretty tough classes here. We're glad that we just have to take notes. You're going to have to interpret them for us," she said.

"I'm glad that she has to take the tests," my mother said. "I haven't been in junior high in over twenty-five years."

It looked like Mrs. Schlitz, Mrs. Graham, and my mother hit it off pretty well. They both had kids in school and understood the predicament that my mother and I were in. I was happy to see that my mother had people with whom she could identify while she spent the day surrounded by thirteen- and fourteen-year-olds.

"Hey, Brooke," said a voice coming from behind Mrs. Schlitz and Mrs. Graham.

"Do you know this young fella, Brooke?" Ms. Calligheris asked. "He's been waiting all morning for you to get here."

When I'm in my wheelchair, I can see only directly in front of me. I can't turn my head from side to side, so my peripheral vision is limited.

"Who's there?" I asked.

"It's me, who did you think, one of the New Kids on the Block?"

It was my friend Michael. Michael and I met that first day I got home from rehab. He was in the crowd of people who were standing under the basketball hoop when the ambulance arrived. He lived on the other side of Nicolls Road and we didn't go to the same elementary school. I didn't know him then, but that changed very quickly. He came to visit me regularly over the summer and we would just hang out and talk. He was one of the only ones who came regularly. Some of the friends that I had before my accident came around when I first came home, but that didn't last very long. I think it was very difficult for them. They knew me the way I used to be and wanted it, as I did, to be like old times. It wasn't and it was difficult for them to accept. Michael knew me no other way. He accepted me just the way I was and I loved him for that.

"Hi, Michael, aren't you supposed to be in homeroom?" I asked.

"Yeah, don't worry, I got a pass. What did you think, I wasn't going to meet you on your first day."

I knew he didn't have a pass and he was cutting out of homeroom. I didn't want him to get in trouble, but I was so glad to see him. He picked up my school bag and blue medical duffel bag and threw one over each shoulder.

"I got these, Mrs. Ellison, why don't we get you to home-room," he said.

"What, are you the only one allowed to cut?" I said with a smile.

He didn't say anything, just grinned, and proceeded to escort all of us down the hall.

Michael helped me overcome the fears I had that first day. He stood by me and was going to make sure no one hurt me. He was a friend, a true friend. He was another Michael in my life.

JEAN

I HAD LONG GROWN out of the adolescent body that the desks in junior high were designed for. Getting into those desks was like trying to squeeze a champagne cork back into an already opened bottle. I stuck out like a woman in the men's locker room. Remaining relatively inconspicuous was something I had to try to do, though, not for me but for Brooke. It was difficult enough for her to have to travel from class to class in her wheelchair with an entourage of people carrying books and carting medical supplies; I didn't want my presence to complicate matters. Our legal appeal to get the district to provide nursing was now at the New York State Court of Appeals. I didn't know how long this situation was going to last, but for as long as it did, I had to draw a delicate balance between being there for Brooke when she needed me and trying to remain invisible the rest of the time. Sailing a forty-year-old boat in a sea of thirteen-year-olds was a challenge.

The teachers, administrators, and kids at Murphy were terrific, and as much as the situation was at times awkward, I enjoyed being in that setting. I wasn't the teacher but I loved the school atmosphere. I would often imagine myself in front of the class-room and was frustrated when I saw things that I thought could be changed. Remaining silent when I wanted to speak out was sometimes very difficult. I didn't want to embarrass Brooke and I had to remember that I was the nurse, not the teacher. In the classroom, I didn't exist unless Brooke needed me.

Not all of the teachers were comfortable with Brooke in the classroom. Unfortunately, we don't live in a perfect world where everybody always does the right thing. It was a lesson that was taught to Brooke early, but it was one she had to learn. English was Brooke's last class of the day, and it was her favorite subject. She loved reading, even though someone had to turn the pages of a book for her, and she loved writing, despite the fact that it was done primarily through dictation. Reading was one of Brooke's windows to the world and writing was an outlet she used to express herself.

In my attempt to make myself invisible in the classroom, I unfortunately must have made Brooke invisible as well. As far as her ninth grade English teacher was concerned, Brooke didn't seem to exist. Brooke always sat by the door so she could leave quickly if there was an emergency. Her teacher would stand on the opposite side of the room and rarely, if ever, make eye contact with her. At first we thought it was just initial nervousness, but as time went by it became clear that she was having a problem with Brooke being in her class.

"It's like I'm not even in the room, Mom," Brooke said to me one afternoon after the class had ended. "I love reading and writ-ing, but I don't want to go to that class anymore. I know I *look* different, but when I'm in that class, she really makes me *feel* different."

"You know, Brooke, when you were in rehab for eight months

you were surrounded by kids with similar problems and adults who were used to dealing with them. When you got home, we couldn't go anywhere because we didn't have a van and you saw only the people who wanted to come to see you. Going back to school is your first experience in the real world since the accident. You are going to meet all kinds of people, and they're not all going to know how to react to you."

"Why is it harder for some adults to accept me than it is for the kids? I was worried how my friends would react; I didn't think I would have a problem with any teachers. She doesn't like me and she doesn't even know me."

"I don't know if it's that she doesn't like you," I said. "I think it's more complicated than that. If you were to ask her, I'd be willing to bet that she doesn't even know what she's doing to you, or if she does know, couldn't explain why. This is something that you are going to experience," I said. "It's up to you how you're going to handle it."

"What do you think it is?" Brooke asked.

"Fear," I said.

"She's afraid of me?"

"Yes, in a way," I said. "This has been going on for thousands of years. People are often afraid of those they perceive as different. That fear can be manifested in many ways. Sometimes it's subtle and sometimes it's much more obvious."

"What can I do about that?"

"You are already doing something. You're out here where people can see you. It's like a cold, you don't get it unless you're exposed to it. That's why it's most important that you go to that class and learn what you can. But I want you to see yourself as the teacher, not the student. She has as much to learn from you as you do from her."

Brooke went to class, and although it appeared that her teacher might have gotten the sniffles, it was never really clear whether she ever caught the cold. Brooke, on the other hand, read wonderful books by Dickens and plays by Shakespeare but learned a much more valuable lesson about life.

BROOKE

"IT'S ME, ANYBODY HOME?"

I heard the side door open and familiar footsteps coming down the hall. It was Deneen, my occupational therapist. My mother and I had just gotten home from school and I was in the den studying. I had my books propped up on a music stand that stood straight up in front of my wheelchair. The books, as usual, were right in front of my face.

"Perfect timing, Deneen, can you turn the page for me?" I said.

"Sure, I'll turn ten pages for you if you want, babydoll," she said.

"One would be nice, but I sure wish I could read ten pages at a time," I said.

"Don't you ever stop studying, your eyes are going to pop right out of your head," she said.

It must have looked like I was studying all the time, not only to Deneen but to anyone who came to the house, and I guess I always was. I studied in bed in the morning while my mother got me dressed before school. I studied when I got home before dinner and after dinner before I went to bed. I studied in bed until I couldn't stay awake any longer, and when I woke up, I started again. The problem was that it took me so much longer than everyone else to do an assignment. If I had to write an essay or a report, I would have to dictate it to someone else. If I had math problems to do, I would have to figure them out in my head and then tell someone what to write down. I couldn't flip back and forth through the pages of a book either, so I had to really concentrate on each page when it came along. I always had to take advantage of whatever time was available to me or I'd never get anything done. It took up just about all my free time.

"I'm sorry, Deneen, I hope you don't think I'm being rude if I continue to read," I said.

"Oh no, you keep reading. I'll massage your neck and turn the pages for you. We're going to get you set up on a voice-activated computer. The technology is much better than it used to be and I think it will help you a lot."

Deneen had been my occupational therapist since I started school in the eighth grade. She was in her twenties, was married but hadn't started a family yet. She had so much energy and excitement about life that it was always fun to be around her. I loved it when she came to work with me, and she had already become a part of our family.

"Hey, Deneen," my mother called from the laundry room where she was folding clothes.

"Hey, Mama, looks like Brookie's finishing up pretty strong. I sure as heck can't keep up with the subjects she's studying here," Deneen shouted.

"Neither can I, and I go to school with her every day. I can't even get her to take a break," my mother said, walking out of the laundry room and over to Deneen to give her a kiss.

"I can't believe she's finishing junior high and going up to the high school already," Deneen said. "Where did the time go?"

"I don't know," my mother said. "If I blink my eyes twice, she'll be in college."

I really didn't know where the time had gone either. Days had turned to weeks and weeks to months and here I was. My father always says that life is like running a marathon. The only way you can get to the finish line is by putting one foot in front of the other. I wasn't really sure where the finish line was, but I was sure I was only a couple of miles into the race.

"Do you miss Michael?" Deneen asked.

"Yes, very much. Ninth grade wasn't the same without him there," I said.

Michael's parents had taken him out of public school and he went to a local private school when we started the ninth grade. I didn't get to see him as much as I used to and that upset me.

"Have you been hanging around with anyone else lately? How about that boy David you were telling me about?"

"I don't know, we were in a lot of classes together this year and we're going to be in a lot together in high school, but . . . I don't know."

It seemed that I had a lot of guy friends—not boyfriends, but guy friends. It was interesting that for some reason guys felt much more comfortable around me than girls did. Guys had no trouble talking to me about just about anything, whereas girls couldn't get past the superficial "Hi, how are ya, gotta go." It was so ironic. Guys now talked to me the way my girlfriends used to and girls now talked to me the way the guys did. I didn't understand it. I loved having guy friends, but I wished that sometimes they could see me as more than just one of the guys.

I was finishing junior high and was doing so much better academically than anyone had ever expected. But I still hadn't gotten the one thing I really wanted to get out of junior high school: a boyfriend.

WE HAD LOST THE CASE against the school board and had exhausted all of our appeals. I had adjusted to the fact that I was not going to be able to return to teaching and would continue on with Brooke until she finished high school. Ed was working, still trying to make ends meet, and was fighting one battle after another with either Medicaid or our health insurance. He spent much of his time appealing rejection letters for services, equipment, and medical supplies. We both thought that dealing with Brooke's physical condition was going to be our most difficult problem. Little did we know that fighting legal battles and handling administrative disputes would be equally as exhausting.

Reed and Kysten were trying to adjust to the new family dynamic and were doing as well as they could. Kysten was still having more difficulty than Reed, though, and was never able to go back to dancing school. Both she and Reed did return to karate, however, and they were both close to getting their black belts. Kysten was still troubled by Brooke's situation and it was taking her longer to accept it. She had difficulty dealing with change and wanted things to be the way they used to be. The fact that Brooke and I would be going up to the high school would be a help to her because we would be seeing a lot more of each other. Brooke was going to be a sophomore and Kysten was starting her senior year. We had even managed to schedule a class together. All three of us were going to be taking French.

After Brooke's accident, there was an interesting transformation in her relationship with Reed. Growing up, they had always been very close, but Brooke had always looked after him. She was his protector, his little mother. From the first day that Brooke arrived home from the hospital, however, those roles reversed. When they were home together, Reed would sit by her side. He would turn the pages of her books and transcribe her assignments, or they would just sit together and talk or play games. He would feed her, scratch an itch if she had one, and make sure she was comfortable. Reed was a big part of Brooke's new life and was instrumental in her being able to adjust to it. They were often inseparable and he had now become *her* protector.

The transition to high school was not going to be an easy one. We would be in a much bigger school, there would be all new people who didn't know us and the schoolwork was going to be a lot more demanding. Brooke had done a little better in junior high school than just getting through the day, as her father had told her to do. She finished with the highest grade point average in the school. This gave her the opportunity to continue with her honors curriculum and also to be placed in the science research class, known as West Prep. This course, which spanned all three years of high school, involved doing science research projects and culminated in the senior year with a submission to the prestigious Westinghouse Science Talent Search. It was highly competitive and intense, but Brooke was very excited about getting in.

Just before the end of ninth grade, Brooke and I went up to the high school to check it out. We needed to see the layout. The high school was the mirror image of the junior high, constructed in red brick with white pillars, but it was at least three times the size. We needed to see if there were any problems that needed to be addressed before we started in September. We met with Brooke's new guidance counselor, Mr. McGaley, who gave us a

tour of the place. Mr. McGaley was a handsome man in his early
thirties. He had a preppie look about him—penny loafers, chinos,
and a pale blue button-down oxford shirt with a maroon tie. He
had a nice clean way about him and a great smile. He and Brooke
hit it off immediately. I was so happy that Brooke's first contact
at the high school was a good one. She was apprehensive and he
was able to put her at ease. We met with the two school nurses,
Barbara Walker and Sue Loverro. The nurses' office was going to
be our home base. There was a little room in the back where
Brooke and I could regroup during the day and I could take care
of some of Brooke's personal needs. Watching Barbara and Sue
work was like watching an Abbott and Costello routine. Barbara
played off Sue, who was like a straight man, but they were both
funny and kept us laughing the entire time we were there. I know
they had never dealt with a situation like Brooke's before, but
they welcomed us without reservation. I knew I was going to get
along well with both of them.

Aside from a couple of narrow doorways and the fact that, in
case of fire, all of Brooke's classes had to be scheduled on the first
floor, things were shaping up pretty well.

"Let's check out the West Prep room," Brooke said just before
we were ready to leave. "Maybe I can get a chance to meet Mrs.
Krieger."

Mrs. Krieger was the director of the program and had established a very formidable reputation for herself through her students' success in the Westinghouse competition. The West Prep
room was close to the nurses' office, so we decided to go by and
take a look. When we entered the room, we could tell that this
class was going to be different. It wasn't a standard classroom; it
had no desks. There was a table with some chairs around it and

a big couch in the corner, where students were lying down and listening to music. There were gadgets of all kinds strewn all over the floor, parts of computers in the back, and, most strange, a soda and candy machine standing against the wall.

Mrs. Krieger came out from the back of the room and after an initial hesitance to approach Brooke, came over.

"You must be Brooke," she said, nodding her head, assessing the situation.

"Yes, I am, and you must be Mrs. Krieger," Brooke said

She was a short, slight woman, with very short salt-and-pepper hair. Her appearance, though, was by no means reflective of her personality. Mrs. Krieger was tough and she laid down the law of the West Prep class to Brooke right away.

"I don't accept late papers and never give any extensions," she said sternly. "Like I tell all of my students, I don't care if you are in the hospital or at death's door, a deadline is a deadline. And you are going to be treated just like everyone else; you'll get no special treatment. Frankly, Brooke, I'm really not sure whether you're going to be able to handle this program. There're going to be a lot of hands-on things that you probably won't be able to do. This class may not work out for you. We'll give it a try if you really want to, but I won't be surprised if it doesn't work out."

She turned away to work with one of her other students and Brooke and I left and went out into the hall. Brooke had always gotten her assignments in on time and had never asked for extensions. That was one of the things that she felt she had to prove. She hated preferential treatment and never asked for it. I couldn't understand what that was all about. When I looked at Brooke, I saw that she was ashen.

"Mom, I don't know if I'm going to be able to do that class,"

Brooke said. "Maybe Mrs. Krieger's right. I don't know if it's going to work out. Maybe I should drop West Prep before I get in too deep."

"Absolutely not," I said. "You've been through this before. You've got nothing to prove, but people have preconceived notions, and unless they're shown differently, nothing changes. This is just another class where you're going to have to be the student and the teacher."

"I don't know, Mom."

"I do, Brooke. It's going to be fine. Remember what your father always tells you when you come up against things like this: 'After all you've been through, this is small potatoes.' "

We went down the hall and out of the building and I wasn't sure what Brooke was going to do. I knew she was upset, but I hoped she would see this situation as she had so many others before: as a motivator, just another obstacle that she had to overcome. She needed to do this not only for herself but for anyone else who might experience what she experienced.

BROOKE

"PSSST, MOM, what's for dinner tonight?" I heard Kysten whisper across the aisle to my mother in the middle of French class.

My mother, not hearing her or not wanting to disrupt the class, didn't respond.

"Mom," Kysten whispered again, only this time more audible to the rest of the class.

"Mademoiselle Kysten, do you have a question that you would like to share with the rest of the class?" my French teacher asked my sister.

He had to use our first names because with all three of us in the class, it was the only way any of us knew who he was talking to.

"No," Kysten said, a little embarrassed. "I only wanted to know what was for dinner tonight."

"Well, Madame Jean, what is for dinner tonight?" he said.

"My husband's cooking tonight, so if I were you, I'd bet the ranch that it's pizza," my mother said.

"Your husband can make pizza?" my French teacher asked.

"No, but he can buy it as well as anyone I know," she said.

Being in high school with my mother was working out pretty well. The kids in school had become accustomed to her presence, and it didn't take long for her to fit in. In addition to becoming good friends with the two school nurses, she was also able to make friends with some of the teachers and grew close to some of the women who worked with me. Maureen Flynn, Martha Goldstein, and Nancy Ryan were all involved in handling some aspect of my special education needs. Mrs. Goldstein and Mrs. Ryan had taken over the responsibilities of Mrs. Schlitz and Mrs. Graham from the junior high. They were my note takers and went to classes with my mother and me during the day. They were as different in personality as Mrs. Schlitz and Mrs. Graham were in appearance. Mrs. Goldstein was forthright and assertive while Mrs. Ryan was quiet and passive. Mrs. Flynn was Ms. Calligheris's counterpart, and it seemed to me that having uncontrollable excitement must have been a prerequisite for that job. She had every bit as much energy as Ms. Calligheris, and she could have been a stand-up comedian as well. There was a very good balance between all of them, and both my mother and I felt blessed for having them in our lives.

Once my mother realized that she was going to be in this

situation for the long haul she started to carve a little niche for herself. She organized little get-togethers that would be held in the nurses' office. One week it would be a "make your own sundae" party and another it would be "potluck." She and the nurses would plan holiday events, and of course we both always dressed up for Halloween. These gatherings grew over time and eventually attracted not only other students and teachers but the assistant principal and principal as well. The school nurses eventually dubbed her the "social director" and had a sign made up saying just that, which they proceeded to put on the door of our little room. She was able to adjust to the many different roles she had to play. She went from mother to nurse and from teacher to student, rarely missing a beat.

Her social life was intertwined with mine, but mine primarily followed hers. We were always together and I became involved with her friends. My social life, however, remained primarily status quo. I would see old friends in the hallway as I traveled from class to class, and they would stop to say hello, but it always remained on a very superficial level. As conspicuous as I was, I still seemed invisible to many. This upset me and I wanted to know what it was that was making people, especially old friends, feel so awkward around me. I tried to put myself in their position in an attempt to get a sense of what it was all about. I thought that maybe my wheelchair was in some way intimidating to everyone. I wondered if it was because my mother was always nearby, but she always gave me the space I needed if I wanted to talk or be with friends. It was obviously something more than that. I got the sense that some people were frightened of me and that I was a reminder of how fragile their own lives really were. I remembered what my mother had said about people's fear of those who were different. I wrote about it in an essay for Mr. McAuliffe's eleventh grade honors English class:

Does anybody really know me? Oh, I know that people know who I am, but does anybody really know me? So often we are defined by the things that we least want to be known for. It is so intriguing how we can see ourselves so differently than how others see us. Our identities can be established for us based on what we look like, what we believe in or what we do for a living. None of these things are likely to give a clue as to what a person is really about. It is much easier for us to see each other in simple terms like this. It requires work to really get to know someone. Sometimes we don't even take the time to really get to know ourselves.

Who am I? I'm the girl on a respirator and in a wheelchair. Is that really me, or is it just what you see? I'm still the same girl I always was. I have the same hopes, the same desires and the same dreams that I always had. I'm a dancer, oh, how I loved to dance. I'm a cellist. I'm a lover of all things beautiful: nature, art, friendship, a kind word. I love music, all kinds of music: rock, classical, hip hop, rap, anything that will stir my soul. I love to touch, be touched, hug and be hugged, and to hold hands. I love a good joke, and it can even be dirty. Don't make fun of anybody, though. I love a good movie. One that will make me laugh or one that will make me cry. But don't let me see anybody get hurt.

We are too complicated to endeavor to label each other with a word. How unfair. We need to take the time. We need to care enough to know, before we decide on what we see. An airplane doesn't get smaller as it flies toward the horizon and I am not defined by my chair. When you see me, look through the metal and the equipment and say hello. I'd like to know who you are, and I'd also like you to know who I really am.

Mr. McAuliffe decided to run the essay in the school newspaper and it was picked up by a local community paper, as well. It was interesting and I don't think it was a coincidence, but people began to stop to talk to me. I hoped that I had broken a barrier for people to not only see me but to see anyone they perceived as "different" in a way that would bring all of us closer together.

JEAN

BROOKE SEEMED DRIVEN. Getting her to slow down was like trying to stop a race car on its way to the finish line. I was in her backseat holding on for dear life. Brooke was starting her senior year and I thought I could see the checkered flag in the distance. She was taking all honors courses and as many advanced college placement courses as she could. She was running an A plus average and had done very well on her SATs. All of her friends were starting to talk about going away to college and it was beginning to upset her because she really couldn't participate in the conversation.

From the day that Brooke returned to school in the eighth grade, both Ed and I felt that if she got through high school and did all right, she would wind up at the State University at Stony Brook. It was an excellent school and it was practically sitting in our own backyard. Kysten was starting her second year there and it was where Brooke had done her Westinghouse Science research over the summer. She was familiar with the campus layout and it was easy for us to get there. Ed and I had talked with Brooke throughout high school about her going there, but I never got the sense from her that it was where she wanted to go.

"What would you think if I said I wanted to go away to school?" Brooke asked me.

"How could we do that, sweetheart?" I said. "Look at how hard it is just getting you through high school."

"We're doing okay, aren't we?" she said. "I'm doing pretty well."

"We can't even get nurses here at home, how would we do it if you were away? That's a really scary thought, Brooke," I said.

"It's not impossible, nothing's really impossible," she said.

"Where would you want to go?" I asked her.

"Maybe Cornell, that's where Carl Sagan teaches. I love Carl Sagan. Or maybe another Ivy League school."

"An Ivy League school," I said in disbelief. "You know your father and I can't afford that."

"Can't we just check it out and see what happens?" she said.

"We'll see, we'll see," I said. "Let me go see if the mail came," I said, trying to change the subject.

"We'll see" was a pat expression that both Ed and I often used to end a discussion with the kids that we thought would certainly result in our having to tell them no. We thought it was a gentler way of letting them down, but I think they hated it when we said that because they felt it was just our way of stalling the inevitable. I know she wanted a straight answer, but I wasn't really in a position to give her one.

"The mail's here, Brooke, and there's a big envelope here addressed to you from Harvard. Was this a setup?" I asked her. "Did you send away for something on the Internet?" Brooke had gotten voice activation computer software that had helped her immensely with her writing, but she was spending a lot of time on the Internet looking at college websites.

"No," she said. "Let me see what it is."

We opened the package and found an application for admission. Apparently colleges send out applications to prospective students based on a review of their SAT scores. Brooke's were good, so Harvard sent her an application.

"This must be a sign," she said.

"What do you mean?"

"We were just talking about this. Don't you think this is a sign telling me that I should apply?"

"I don't know, but I think there's a dollar sign telling you not to."

"C'mon, I'm serious. What's the harm in just applying? I probably won't get in."

"It's the fact that you might that scares me," I said.

"If I get in, I'll frame the acceptance letter and put it on the wall," she said. "It will give us something to talk about."

"Okay," I said. "I'll talk to your father, I'm pretty sure it will be okay with him."

"I can't believe it," Brooke said.

"It's only the application, honey. Don't get too excited."

"No, I can't believe you said 'we'll see,' and it didn't turn out to be a 'no.' Wait till Reed hears this."

Ed and I talked about it and we both felt that there would be no real harm in her just applying. Brooke and I put together the application package and gave it to Mr. McGaley, who attached her transcript and letters of recommendation. She decided that she would apply to only two schools: Harvard, for early admission, and Stony Brook later on in the year.

"Do you think I have a chance, Mr. McGaley?" Brooke asked.

"As good as anybody else," he said matter-of-factly.

"Do you really think so?" I asked him. He and Brooke were a mutual admiration society, so I didn't know whether I should take him seriously.

"Oh yeah, she's very competitive," he said again with assurance.

At that point, I didn't know what to think. I told her that she had to realize that the chances of her getting into Harvard were remote and that she shouldn't get her hopes up. "It's always better to be pleasantly surprised than bitterly disappointed," I told her. She said that she had no expectations about getting in, but wouldn't I be proud of her if she did.

That was the problem. What if she did get in? How would we handle that? Could we tell her to apply and then, if she got in, tell her she couldn't go?

I had made a commitment after Brooke's accident that if I couldn't change her physical situation, I would do everything in my power to try to improve the quality of her life. No matter what it took. It didn't seem that her going away to school would be possible, but I wondered whether the checkered flag I thought I saw was signaling the end of a race or was just a sign that a new one was about to begin.

BROOKE

I MET DAVID back in my eighth grade earth science class. Dr. Brooks had asked all of us to get together with a partner because we were starting a new lab on rocks. Those situations are always uncomfortable, and with my circumstances I worried whether anyone would want to work with me. An awkward-looking kid with dark hair and glasses came over to me from across the room. The only thing bigger than his smile was his feet. They had obviously grown much faster than the rest of his body, and he shuffled them when he walked. He was wearing sneakers and a T-shirt that said across the front: BAD SPELLERS OF THE WORLD UNTIE.

"Hi, Brooke, I'm David. Do you want to work with me?" he said. "I'm no good at rocks but maybe we can figure something out together."

"I don't know anything either," I said, "but I'm willing to give it a shot."

I wasn't sure how we would work together, but I was certainly open to getting to know someone new. I invited him over to the house that afternoon so that we could work on the lab. When David came by he was at first a little unsure of himself and was at times self-deprecating. He referred to himself as a nerd. I didn't know if that was courageous or just plain stupid. I knew that he was the kind of kid who got picked on in school, and I couldn't understand why he would want to give anyone any additional ammunition. I know that when you identify yourself with an epithet that others use against you as an insult, it removes its power. In David's case, though, I got the feeling it was a label that he was proud of. We worked on the lab and I found that he was not only smart but had a quick, intellectual sense of humor. He made me laugh, and I liked that. We hit it off right away.

From that afternoon on, my friendship with David grew. We were in a lot of classes together and spent a lot of time with each other at school. He would come by the house and visit and we would talk on the phone. We often worked on projects together, talked about our common interests in baseball and politics, played games, and watched movies. Our friendship grew closer all through high school and we really enjoyed each other's company. He would sit by my side, play with my hair, and hold my hand. He and I became best friends.

At the beginning of our senior year, we both applied for early admission to Harvard and David also asked me to the prom. He wanted to ask me early because we were such close friends and he couldn't imagine going with anyone else. He thought that we would have a really good time together. I was very flattered by his asking me, but I wasn't sure how I was going to handle it. I was facing some conflicting emotions; I wanted to go, but I didn't know how much my not being able to dance at the prom would upset me. I was also hesitant to accept David's offer so early because I didn't want him to feel obligated to me if something was to change before the prom arrived. I told him that we should wait a little while before making that decision.

With each passing week, David asked me again and again about the prom. I would reiterate my concerns; he would dismiss them and tell me not to worry. "We'll have a great time," he'd tell me. In the beginning of December, just before the early admission decisions came in, David asked me one more time and I finally said yes. I told him I would go with him. We were both excited and I was looking forward to making plans and picking out a dress.

The whole college admissions process was extremely stressful for many of my friends. That and the Westinghouse competition were the only subjects of conversation for weeks. David, in particular, seemed very anxious and couldn't talk about anything else. It was an exciting time, but I couldn't understand where all the pressure was coming from. Was it from parents or was it just pure competition? I was in a very competitive academic program in school and I think that a lot of the kids in it viewed a college acceptance notice the same way a good athlete viewed scoring a winning touchdown or a basket in a championship game. It was a win, a victory for yourself and at times a triumph over everyone else who didn't get in. It didn't make a lot of sense to me. It may have been because of all that I had been through after my accident, or what I had to deal with just to get through each day, but getting into college didn't have the same sense of urgency for me as it did for everyone else. I was enjoying the excitement but I hated the anxiety.

December 15 was the day the early admissions decisions were expected from Harvard. If you wanted to know whether or not you got in you had one of two options. You could wait for a letter to come in the mail or you could call the admissions office in Cambridge to find out. I was going to wait for a letter.

"Did you call Harvard yet, Brooke?" Mrs. Krieger asked when she saw me in the hall. She knew full well what the process was and when the decisions would be available.

"No, I think that I'm going to wait for the letter," I said.

"Okay," she said, almost disappointed.

I was beginning to feel some of the anxiety that everybody was talking about. My friends and teachers who knew that I had applied to Harvard, and even Mr. McKean, the school principal, wanted to know if I had heard. I decided I wouldn't wait, and told my mother and Mrs. Krieger that I was going to call.

From the nurses' office, my mother dialed the number of admissions at Harvard and held the phone to my ear. I couldn't believe what I was feeling. In my head I was calm and thought that I held this situation in the right perspective, but in my gut I was scared to death.

"Harvard admissions office," I heard on the other end of the line. I swallowed hard and tried to say something. Nothing came out.

"Harvard admissions office," I heard again.

"Oh, yes, I'm sorry, my name is Brooke Ellison and I'm calling for the results of my application," I said.

"Hello, Brooke. We need some identification first. What is your Social Security number, your SAT score, and the score of your last achievement test?" the admissions officer asked.

I rattled off some numbers almost unconsciously and bit my bottom lip before she gave a response. There was a pause that lasted probably only a few seconds, but it seemed to be in biblical time, where a second is a hundred years.

"Welcome to the Harvard Class of 2000, Brooke. Congratulations," she said.

"My goodness, thank you so much!" My face turned bright red and I started to cry. "I got in, I got in," I said to my mother almost in disbelief.

My mother hung up the phone and she started to cry, too. I couldn't believe what had just happened or what I was feeling. What I had downplayed up till then had become one of the most exciting moments in my life. I was euphoric. I felt that my acceptance to Harvard was a validation and a recognition of all the hard work that both my mother and I had done over the past six years. Harvard wanted me and I felt that I had proved something, not just to myself but to anyone who thought I couldn't or shouldn't do it. I couldn't wait to tell my father and I couldn't wait to tell David.

BROOKE CALLED HER FATHER at work immediately after she told me; she wanted to make sure he was the next one to know. I got on the phone with him after she told him the news.

"What do you think about that?" I said in amazement.

"As soon as I pick myself up off the floor, I'll tell you," he said.

"It's wonderful, isn't it?" I said. "She's stunned and she's so happy."

"It's incredible," he said, "but what are we going to do now? How are we going to do this?" he said.

The bell rang to change classes and we had to get to West Prep.

"We gotta go," I said. "But we have a lot to talk about when you get home."

"I know, we'll talk later. Kiss Brooke for me and give yourself one, too. I love you guys," he said, "good job."

Brooke and I took off for class, and when we entered West Prep, we heard Mrs. Krieger shout from across the room: "Well, did you call? Have you heard anything?"

Brooke's cheeks were still red and she had a huge smile on her face and she didn't need to say a word. Mrs. Krieger came running across the room and gave her a big kiss on her forehead.

"Congratulations! You're Harvard bound," she said with certainty.

She said it as if it was just going to happen and nothing more needed to be said about it.

"I don't know how we're going to do it," I said, trying to send a message that no decision had been made yet as to whether she was actually going to go.

"She can do anything," Mrs. Krieger said without a moment's hesitation.

I was reminded of how far both she and Brooke had come since that first meeting back in the ninth grade. Mrs. Krieger had written a letter of recommendation to Harvard for Brooke and she had become one of Brooke's biggest advocates. Brooke had finished and submitted her Westinghouse project and had done many different research projects in the years she was in Mrs. Krieger's class. All of them were submitted on time. She encouraged Brooke to be a member of her academic competition team, which competed against other schools. It was like the game show *Jeopardy!*, where team members pressed a buzzer when they thought they knew the answer to a question. The student who pressed the button first got to answer the question. Brooke couldn't use her hands, so they devised a buzzer that was activated by a switch she controlled with her chin. It made it possible for her to compete. Brooke learned so much from Mrs. Krieger, but I think Mrs. Krieger was taught something by Brooke as well. They were both students and they were both teachers and they developed a beautiful relationship that was based on mutual respect and admiration.

The kids from West Prep gathered around Brooke and congratulated her. Her good friend Seth, who was so happy for her, wrote in big letters across the blackboard: BROOKE WAS ACCEPTED TO HARVARD!

Brooke looked around for David and saw him leaning against the wall in the back of the room. When they made eye contact, David walked over slowly with his head down, apparently disappointed, and softly said, "Congratulations." He left the room without saying another word. He didn't talk to her in class after that and didn't call her on the telephone. He avoided her in the hall and never came to the house again to visit. Brooke was upset, confused, and disappointed. A prom date was canceled and a friendship was ended over a college admission.

BROOKE

WHEN MY MOTHER AND I CAME HOME from rehab five years earlier, we made a vow as a family never to split up again. It had been so difficult living apart that just the thought of ever doing it again was painful. The possibility of going away to Harvard was exciting, but the thought of actually doing it scared me. It was a decision I couldn't make for myself because it wasn't just about me; the impact would be felt by every member of the family. When I applied to Harvard, I really didn't entertain any thoughts of actually going. I really thought that if, by some strange twist in my already peculiar and complicated life, I did get accepted, I would just frame the letter, put it on the wall, and, when I looked at it, fantasize about what it might have been like to actually go there. I knew how difficult life was for my parents and how hard they were trying to make life better for me. I knew this wouldn't be just another "we'll see" answer that they would ultimately dismiss. I knew that if they thought going to Harvard would improve my life, they would do everything possible to make it happen. I felt guilty, guilty for having applied in the first place and guilty for having put them in this position. I asked Reed what he thought.

"You have to go, Brookie," he said without hesitation. "These opportunities don't come around very often."

"What if Mom went with me?" I asked him, trying to address my biggest concern right away. "This is going to be your junior year, a big year for you. You have your Westinghouse to do, your music, we'd miss all of your concerts."

"I'd miss you guys, but you still have to do it . . . except for just one thing, though. Dad would be doing all the cooking, wouldn't he? That might be more than I could handle," he said.

He and I both laughed, but I knew Reed really meant what he said about my going. Yet I also knew how difficult this would be to do, and how hard it would be on everyone. Aside from the financial questions, obviously I couldn't afford to go to Harvard with just my father working; there were so many other issues that would have to be resolved.

First and foremost, I would need to have someone up in Cambridge with me at all times. As it was at home, we only had Debby a few days a week and another nurse, Michele, who came during the week, in the evening. Getting enough nurses to cover twenty-four hours a day, seven days a week would be very unlikely. The only person I could depend on to be with me was my mother. Could she possibly go away to college with me? It would mean splitting up the family again. She didn't even go away to college herself when she was my age, and my father transferred home after only one year because he didn't want to be away from her. I didn't know if I could ask my mother or anyone in my family to do that.

There were so many other issues to think about. If my mother was to go away with me, how would she be able to handle being up there alone without the support system we had at home? She and my father always did everything together and he was her relief. It wasn't just a question of whether I could handle being away from home; we also had to consider whether my mother could deal with being away from the family as well. I didn't know whether Harvard would even allow someone else to come with me, let alone it being my mother. How would they provide enough living space for two people?

Then there were the many logistical issues to contend with. We would have to try to duplicate at Harvard what we had at home. I would need a ventilator, a hospital bed, a lift to get me in and out of bed, and medical supplies would have to be sent up there on a regular basis. We would have to have at least a month's supply on hand at all times. I would have to find a doctor up there and have special transportation available to get me where I needed to go. How would we be able to do all that? There were so many things that we had to consider, and the more I thought about it, the more unlikely it seemed that I would ever be able to go.

After a long family discussion, we decided that we would at least look into the possibility. We decided to approach it the same way we did the application itself. We felt that, just like there was no harm in applying to Harvard, there would be no harm in investigating the possibility of my being able to attend. My father contacted the Harvard admissions office, and when he spoke to them, he asked if they were fully aware of the problems that I faced. He went on to tell them of the extent of my physical situation and truly expected that that would be the end of our investigation. We all thought that I would ultimately wind up attending Stony Brook University in the fall. The admissions office assured him, however, that they were aware of my situation and that they were excited at the prospect of having me as a student. I still don't think my father believed them.

A trip to Cambridge was arranged to look at the campus, meet with administrators, voice our concerns, and figure out whether it was really possible for me to become a Harvard student. I wasn't really sure how everyone felt about this. Reed said I should go and my parents were giving it their best effort, but I didn't know if any of them really believed it could actually happen. Kysten was the least enthusiastic and maybe the most honest. She was just getting used to the way our lives were at home, and the thought of having to adjust to this new situation upset her. She was a homebody, didn't like change, and really couldn't understand why I would ever want to leave the area, especially with Mom and my circumstances. I think she thought I was a little bit crazy. The thought entered my mind that maybe she was right.

JEAN

IN LATE FEBRUARY, Ed, Reed, Debby, and I made the five-and-a-half-hour trip up to Cambridge with Brooke. We stayed at a hotel on the Charles River and it was the first time since Brooke had come home from the hospital five years earlier that she had spent the night away from home. We arrived at the hotel on Tuesday night and were scheduled to have a meeting the next day with Elizabeth Nathans, the freshman dean; Louise Russell from the disabilities office; and a representative from health services. The night that we arrived, the sun had not yet set and I was looking out the window of the hotel with Debby. The Charles was still partially frozen and the setting sun was reflecting off the ice. I could see the Harvard campus across the river. There were students jogging along the riverbank, and I could see the Harvard boathouse in which the crew team stored its boats.

"Brooke has to be able to come here," I said to Debby. "Look at that," I said, pointing across the river at the campus. "It's so beautiful."

"I know, but we haven't heard what they have to say yet," she said. "It would be nice, though."

In the five years that Debby had been with us, we had become like sisters. She shared in all our family's joys and all of our sorrows and we shared in hers, as well. She and her husband, John, had difficulty conceiving a child and two years earlier decided to go through the in vitro fertilization procedure. I gave her the shots that she needed to take throughout the process and the procedure worked. She gave birth to a boy they named Zachary and she asked Brooke to be his godmother. This was also her first time spending the night away from home without Zach.

None of us slept very much that night. There are always worries about Brooke's equipment, and being in an unfamiliar setting heightened those concerns. We also didn't know what to expect from the meeting the next day. And, of course, there was also the excitement of being up at Harvard. Harvard was a place we had all only heard about or seen in the movies; there was a mystique about it that was exciting. If nothing else came from this trip, we thought, at least we would have had the opportunity to see the place.

Our meeting was scheduled for ten o'clock in the morning, and a Harvard shuttle bus was arranged to pick us up at nine-thirty. When we went down to the lobby, there was a beige van with a crimson stripe and the Harvard insignia waiting outside. Pacing between the van and the door of the hotel was a man dressed in khaki pants, tasseled loafers, and a navy blue sport jacket. I thought he was one of the deans. We went to the door and he introduced himself: "I'm your ride," he said. He looked at Brooke and said, "I'm Cahl, head of the Hahvid shuttle services, and I'm here to be your escort today."

"Nice to meet you, I'm Brooke," she said. "I'm here, and I'm a little nervous today."

Reed looked at me and whispered in my ear, "Did you understand him, Mom?"

Carl was in his thirties and had dark hair and glasses and an engaging personality that we all liked. He was clearly a Bostonian.

Ed obviously didn't understand him either, because he kept calling him Cal and didn't realize his name was Carl until I told him well after the damage had been done.

The Harvard shuttle van had a lift in it that was similar to the one we had, but when we tried to get Brooke in, her wheelchair wouldn't fit. There was a seat blocking the way.

"We're going to have to remove those seats in our vans if Brooke's going to come here," he said in all his Boston splendor. "This isn't going to work out," he said. Ed and I looked at each other and I thought to myself, "We haven't even gotten there yet and we already have a problem." We ended up having to take our own van with Carl doing the driving. Ed sat up front with Carl, while Debby, Reed, and I sat in the back with Brooke.

We drove down Harvard Street and Carl was like a tour guide.

"On your left you'll see the Coliseum, where all the football games are played," he said. "You can probably tell how it got its name. It was designed to look just like the Colosseum in Rome. Do you like football, Brooke?" he asked.

"I sure do," she said. "But I don't play."

"We're now on the Harvard Street Bridge and that's the Charles River," he said.

The Charles River was the only thing that looked familiar to us up close.

"We've been looking at the Charles from the hotel," Ed said. "Actually, we're so familiar with it now, we feel pretty comfortable calling it the Chuck."

We crossed the bridge, over Memorial Drive and down J.F.K. Street and into Harvard Square. I could see the excitement in Brooke's face. We turned down Massachusetts Avenue and made a left onto Prescott Street and pulled up in front of a yellow, New England–style clapboard house. It was the freshman dean's office and we were met by Louise Russell from the disabilities office. Louise was a pleasant woman who had already been very helpful and supportive to us. I had spoken to her several times prior to our trip. She was disabled herself and needed to use crutches when she walked. We were happy to see a ramp that led up to a doorway that was wide enough for Brooke to fit through. Louise led us into the conference room where our meeting was to be held. It was a big office with a fireplace and had a large dark wood table with leather chairs around it. It looked exactly like what I thought a Harvard dean's office would look like. Louise Russell introduced us to Elizabeth Nathans, the freshman dean, and told us that everyone around here calls her "Ibby." She was an older woman who wasn't even the slightest bit intimidating. She was soft-spoken, gentle, and had a very maternal way about her. She introduced a woman from health services and two assistant deans. We all gathered around the table.

We had compiled a long list of questions and concerns to address at the meeting. Ed pulled the list out of his briefcase and started with the first. We talked about some of the concessions that would have to be made, and the arrangements that would be necessary. We said that Brooke would need an accessible bathroom. We told them that it would have to be attached to a room that would have to be big enough for her to be able to get around in. We went over each question, and all of our concerns one by one. We were all shocked that every item that we addressed didn't seem to pose any problem. "Accessible bathroom, we can do that. Extra-large room, we can do that, too."

When we came to the biggest issue, the fact that I would probably have to live with Brooke on campus and go with her to all her classes, no one even flinched.

"Mom needs to stay with you? As long as you don't get involved in Brooke's academic business, we can arrange for that as well," they told me.

None of us could believe what we were hearing. Harvard never gave Ed and me a chance to get off the hook. We never had a reason to tell Brooke no. The only problems they could think of were ones that were beyond their control. "The winters are cold," they said, "and the cobblestone sidewalks are slippery in the winter and bumpy all year round. Brooke might have trouble traveling over them," they said. Considering everything that was involved in Brooke's going away to college, I thought these few problems were ones we could certainly live with.

BROOKE

MY FATHER HAD VISITED the financial aid office when we were at Harvard and we didn't hear until March whether we would be able to afford my going up there. Harvard's gracious generosity once again made my decision more difficult. The door was open, but I still knew how difficult it would be for me to go and how much of a strain it would put on my family. I had a dilemma. I wanted to go so much but didn't want to separate my family. Was I being selfish, or was I maximizing my potential as my parents had always told me to do?

My family at this point told me it was now just my decision. My mother was willing to go and give it a try, knowing full well how hard it was going to be on her. My father said it was okay with him as well, but I knew how much he would worry and how much he would miss my mother. Reed still told me that I had to go and even Kysten told me to go if I really wanted to. I still put off my decision. I had until May to decide.

The weeks passed quickly and my family and friends were encouraging me to go. "Try it, even if it's only for a year. If it doesn't work out, you can always come home," they said.

Ironically, it was the naysayers who were really pushing me. It seems that no matter what a person accomplishes, there will always be people who feel diminished by those accomplishments. I don't know where it was coming from, but as is usually the case with these kinds of things, it made its way back to me. Despite the fact that I had an A plus average, a 1510 on my SATs, and had been selected as one of the top twenty academic students in the country by the national newspaper *USA Today*, it was still difficult for some people to accept my admittance to Harvard. Some said I was accepted only because I was in a wheelchair. They felt that I was selected only to fill some mandated disability quota. Others felt that I shouldn't have gotten in because I would be taking an able-bodied person's place. In their minds it was a waste of time and a waste of money for me to go. What was I going to do with a Harvard degree?

The people who pushed me the most, though, weren't the ones who said I shouldn't have gotten in; it was the ones who said I wouldn't succeed if I went. Some said I wouldn't be able to make it because of my physical challenges. Others thought there would be no way I would be able to compete academically up at Harvard. It made me more sad than angry, and I wondered whether these people really knew me or whether they were speaking from some preconceived, uninformed place. I felt that maybe they needed to be educated, and it reminded me of what I had gone through years earlier trying to get back into school.

My good friend Mrs. Rose, Rosie to everyone else who knew her, came to the house for a visit. She was one of the special education tutors at the high school who worked with me when one of my scheduled tutors wasn't available. She came by the house frequently on her own time, always with some goodies and treats to eat, and we studied the Bible together. She was one of the most caring and loving people I had ever met and I loved her and the time we spent together. When she finished her visit, she told me that the school board was considering cutting special education services and that she was in danger of losing her job. I told her I knew about the problem and that the director of special education had asked me to speak to the school board at their next open meeting in support of the services and employees who might get cut. I told Mrs. Rose that at first I was unsure about whether I could speak to the board because of the problems that my family had with them in the past. I told her, though, that I had ultimately agreed to speak, and that I would do anything I could to help the situation.

The crowd at the school board meeting was much larger than normal. There were more parents and teachers and administrators at this meeting because of the wide range of programs that were in danger of being cut. It wasn't just special education that was being affected. There were other programs and services that affected a large cross section of the student population. The meeting was held in the cafeteria of the junior high school and people spilled out into the hallways. With all the people there, I positioned myself up in front so that I wouldn't cause a commotion when it was my turn to speak. I was sitting directly opposite the school board members. I was very nervous, and I realized that this must have been how my father felt when he spoke to them five years earlier. But I knew it was something I had to do. About twenty minutes into the meeting, I was called on to speak:

Five years ago, my father spoke before the school board to try to get the needed services so that I could be mainstreamed back in school after my accident. It's five years later, and now I'm here before you. My purpose is much broader and more serious because I'm not speaking just for myself, I'm speaking on behalf of all the students with special needs who follow me. Why should they have to come down here and fight for the quality, mainstreamed education that they deserve? It shouldn't be denied them due to their individual circumstances, and it certainly shouldn't be denied them based on the design of the school board.

I think that this board needs to look very closely at its sense of priorities and its sense of responsibility to the entire community, and that includes the students with special needs. Yes, we need to be financially responsible, but don't try to balance the budget on the backs of these students. They are part of our future as well. After my accident and resulting disabilities, there were many people who felt that I shouldn't return to a mainstreamed educational setting. Some felt that I should be taught at home, and others felt that I should attend a special school with other students who faced physical challenges. Despite these sentiments, I did return to the mainstream and was given the opportunity to cultivate my abilities. Now, I'm happy to say,

I will graduate this year and the special school that I will be attending in the fall will be Harvard University.

It saddens me to think that there is a possibility that the children with special needs coming through the system now may not have the opportunity to work with the programs, teachers, and tutors that I was so fortunate to have. They are the very best, and they should remain the very best.

I hope that tonight I can help convince this board of the wisdom of preserving the special education programs in this district, and in particular the tutors and support people who work so closely with the students. Without them there is no special education. They make dreams come true.

In closing, I would like to ask all of you on the school board to ask yourselves this one question: How can the parents of the special needs students tell their children to reach for the stars and pursue their dreams if this board decides that they are not worth the financial investment?

Please think about that. Thank you.

For a few seconds after I finished speaking, there was silence. Then the members of the school board stood up and applauded. Some of them were the very same people who, five years earlier, denied my father's requests for help to get me back into school. I really couldn't understand why this was happening. Why were the people I was taking to task giving me a standing ovation? The rest of the crowd stood and joined the school board in their applause.

Maybe we all learned something that night. My perception of them had changed. I could see that they were just people trying to do their jobs the best they could. I hoped that their perception of me had changed, as well. I hoped that I had changed a mind or an attitude, and possibly made it easier for those who might follow me. I also hoped that I had the courage to keep on going because I also realized that night that I had made my decision. I was going to Harvard. I was going there to learn and, who knows, maybe to teach.

PART THREE

Character cannot be developed in ease and quiet.
Only through experience of trial and suffering can the soul be
strengthened, ambition inspired, and success achieved.

—HELEN KELLER

"ARE WE SURE we really want to do this?" I said to Brooke as I added another item to the "things we need to take to Harvard" list that was growing exponentially as the day of our departure rapidly approached. It was beginning to resemble the Dead Sea scrolls. We had to break the list down into sublists. There was the "medical supplies list," the "equipment list," the "clothes list," the "school supply list." There was a list of "people we need to contact at Harvard" and one for the "things we need to do when we get there." I needed a list just to keep track of my lists. I come from the school of thought that believes that "if it's not on a list, it doesn't exist" and "if it hasn't been crossed off, it hasn't been done." It stems from my early beliefs that you can actually have some control over your own life. Even though experience has taught me that it's really only an illusion, I still humor myself on occasion.

The entire summer after high school graduation was spent getting ready to go away. Being so busy was a blessing of sorts because it didn't give me time to dwell on how dramatically different our lives were about to become. I couldn't sit and ponder all the scary "what if" questions either. I kept adding to my lists and crossing items off of them. We had medical equipment, packed boxes of medical supplies, and personal effects stacked up in the garage. It looked like we were either ready to set up a hospital or had just robbed one.

A few days before Brooke was scheduled to be up at school for the beginning of the freshman week festivities, Ed rented a truck to haul everything up to Boston early so that it would be up there when we arrived.

"I hope your father got a big enough truck and rented a couple of the Seven Santini Brothers to help him get all this stuff up to Boston," I said to Brooke.

"He won't need any more help," Brooke said, "he's got Matt."

Matt was Deneen's husband, and through her, he, too, had become a close family friend. He offered to give Ed a hand and go up to Harvard with him. Matt was a big guy, an ex–football player whose heart was as big as his biceps.

Brooke's friend Michael and his parents, Ernie and Deb, came over to help Ed and Matt load the truck. They set up a system like a bucket brigade handing off labeled boxes to each other from the garage, up a ramp, and into the truck.

"Here's a box labeled 'Brooke's shoes,' " Michael said, passing it off to Ed.

"Here's another one," Ernie said, passing this one off to Michael.

"Here's one more," Matt said in disbelief as he gave it to Ernie. "How could you have so many pairs of shoes, Brooke? You could give Imelda Marcos a run for her money."

"I just don't wear them out, Matt," Brooke said. "If you're

jealous, though, I'll let you borrow some. Just let me know if you see a pair you like."

Everyone was trying to keep things light. We were all joking and laughing, but each box and piece of equipment that was loaded onto that truck was a reminder of how close we were to leaving. All summer I had been able to push it to the back of my mind, but now it was staring me in the face. I knew that in just a couple of days, I would have to say good-bye to Reed and Kysten. Saying good-bye wasn't written on any of my lists. Maybe I thought that if I didn't write it down, it wouldn't have to happen and I'd never have to cross it off.

BROOKE

I WOKE UP AND STARED at the angel figurines that lined the shelf on the wall next to my bed. I collected angels, all kinds. Some were made from ceramic and some from cloth. They sat on my doorjambs and hung from my ceiling. They hid inside music boxes and were stitched on the pillows in my room. They were comforting. They watched over me.

It was early and Reed, as always, came into my room before he left for school to say good-bye. This time, though, I knew I wouldn't see him when he got home. The day had finally come. We were leaving and I had to say good-bye.

"Good morning, Brookie," Reed said softly, not sure whether I was awake.

"Good morning, Reed," I said tentatively, not really knowing how I was going to handle the rest of the conversation.

"Are you okay?" he asked.

"I'm okay, but I don't want to say good-bye."

"Then don't," he said. "You don't have to. We'll treat it like any other day, and before you go to sleep tonight, we can talk on the phone."

Reed pulled up a chair and sat next to the bed just like he always did when we talked at night. When I first got home from the hospital he used to stand next to my bed and talk and we would still be eye to eye. He had gotten so tall now that when I was in bed, he had to sit down for me to be able to see him. He was six feet three inches tall and had already gone through all the gawky awkward stages of adolescence. His smile, as always, made me feel good, and his laugh was still infectious. I studied him, and I made another mental photograph for my scrapbook. His long brown hair, parted down the middle, was the only reminder of how he looked when he was little. He wasn't a cute little boy anymore; he was handsome and had become a man.

I was so proud of him—how he handled my accident, and the attention that was given to me and taken from him. How he didn't give Mom and Dad any more trouble than they already had. How he went back to karate when he wanted to quit, and got his black belt. How he stepped up when I needed him, and Lord knows, there were so many times when I did. There were the little things that he did every day without giving them a thought, and then there were the big things that I knew he did that came straight from his heart.

When my senior prom came, I wasn't going to go. There were a lot of people going without dates, but I had vowed to stay home. Reed seemed more upset than I was.

"Would you go with me, Brooke?" he asked. "I know I'm your brother and it probably wouldn't be the same for you, but I would love to take you. That is, only if you want to go with me."

At first I didn't know what to say. Going to the prom with your brother was something you just didn't do, but going to school with your mother wasn't becoming a trend, either. We always did things differently, and besides, what difference did it make? There was no one I loved more or whose company I would rather have.

"It would be my honor to have you escort me," I told him.

We went, and I'm so glad that we did. It's a memory that I will never forget and one that I will always be able to share with one of the most important men in my life.

Reed got up from the chair and told me that he had to go.

"Okay, we won't say good-bye, but I'm going to miss you so much, Reed," I said, breaking the promise I made to myself not to cry.

Reed took a tissue and dabbed the corners of my eyes and wiped my cheeks. "I'm going to miss you, too, Brookie," he said.

"Promise me you'll be careful and you'll work hard in school. Maybe in a couple of years you'll come up to Harvard and join us," I said.

"I promise," he said. He leaned over, kissed me on the forehead, and walked out of the room.

When he left, I didn't know when I would see him again, but I knew he would always be with me. He was more than just my brother; he was my angel.

JEAN

MOST COLLEGES START CLASSES the last week of August or the first week in September. Harvard never really gets started until the third week in September. Ed and Matt drove up on September 3. They left at four in the morning, to beat the traffic, and drove straight up to Cambridge. When they got there, they found that the room was still being renovated. There were tarps down and sawhorses set up on the floor in the middle of the room. Hammers banged while two-by-fours screamed as power saws cut them to pieces on the floor.

"My wife and my daughter are coming up here in a couple of days," Ed shouted over the noise of the power tools.

"Don't worry, we'll be done by then," one of the workmen shouted back with assurance.

Ed's experience was that any construction job, at no matter what stage of completion, was always at least two weeks away from being done.

"Okay," Ed said, doubting what he just heard. "My buddy and I are going to be bringing in some boxes and equipment. We'll try to stay out of your way," he shouted back again.

They unloaded everything from the truck, but couldn't set anything up because of the work that was still being done. They drove home that same day.

"So what did you think of the place?" Ed asked Matt on the way home.

"I feel smarter just having been there," Matt said. "You wouldn't have a book on theoretical linear algebra and multivariable calculus I could read," he said with a smirk.

"No, but I just finished a great book on partial differential and integral equations that I know you would just love," Ed said.

Matt had been reviewing the course catalog that Brooke had gotten over the summer and was having some fun with it. Ed was just trying to keep up with him.

"Seriously, Matt," Ed said, "do you think their rooms will be ready by the time we go back up there?"

"No way," Matt said without even pausing a moment to think about it.

Matt, who had worked a number of years in construction, only reaffirmed what Ed was already thinking.

Freshman orientation week started September 7, and we left on the sixth. Even with the truckload that was sent up earlier, there were still so many last-minute items that had to be packed into the van before we all got in. Debby offered to come with us to help set up the room.

I had said the inevitable good-byes to Kysten and Reed and it was as difficult as I had expected. I told them that I would speak to them every day and they should call me anytime they wanted to. Ed's parents, who had moved closer to us, came to say good-bye. They had both been so supportive of us after Brooke's accident, and Ed's mother, who had taken care of Kysten and Reed while we were in the hospital, was now taking care of her husband. He was suffering from Alzheimer's disease and his condition was getting worse very rapidly. He unfortunately couldn't understand where we were going or what we were doing. He never really got to know what Brooke had accomplished.

The trip from Stony Brook to the ferry at Orient Point took approximately an hour and fifteen minutes. Orient Point was as far east as you could travel on the north shore of Long Island. If you drove any farther you would plunge into the Atlantic Ocean. There was a ferry that left almost every hour on the hour and traveled north across Long Island Sound to New London, Connecticut. It didn't save us much time, but it eliminated having to drive through New York City, which made it a much more pleasant ride. Traveling east on Route 25, we passed the farms that we went to every year in October to pick pumpkins. The U-PICK YOUR OWN signs were already up in anticipation of this year's season. Ed couldn't resist asking Brooke if she thought the signs were really just the farmers' subtle way of insulting all the people driving by in their cars. Brooke, as she always did, rolled her eyes and refused to answer him when she thought he was saying something particularly silly.

We passed the sod farms and potato farms and drove through the vineyards farther out on the east end.

"You can really stretch your eyes out here," I said as we drove along the shoreline, getting closer to Orient Point. "Look at how beautiful that is—the blue sky, the green grass, and the ocean, a blend of them all. It makes you feel good to be alive."

"This is the real Long Island," Ed said. "It's not all the things you read in the newspaper. It's the soil and the water, the farmers and the fishermen that make up the heart and soul of this place. Anybody who doesn't believe that should just take a ride out here."

The beautiful scenery and our thoughts about what we were doing and where we were going made the hour and fifteen minutes pass by very quickly. We pulled up to the ferry, loaded the van on board, and set off on the second leg of the trip. Brooke couldn't get into the passenger cabin, so we all stayed out on the car deck. It was a bright sunny day and still warm, so we all welcomed the opportunity. It was the first time any of us had been out on a boat since before Brooke's accident, when we all used to sail on Ed's sister Margaret's and her husband Lee's sailboat. The bright sun reflecting off the water, the cool breeze on our faces, and the smell of salt in the air gave us all a wonderful feeling of freedom.

"Let it blow, Mom," Brooke said to me when I started to pull her hair back into a ponytail. "It's moving, and it makes me feel like I'm moving," she said. "It feels wonderful and exhilarating."

I left her alone and sat down next to Ed and Debby.

"How's she doing?" Ed said.

"Look at the smile on her face," I said, and took my hair down to let it blow freely in the wind.

BROOKE

AS WE TURNED ONTO HARVARD STREET, I felt like someone came up from behind and startled me. My heart was racing, my stomach was dancing, and my adrenaline was flowing. I could see the Coliseum on the left and the playing fields on the right. Things were beginning to look familiar from the trip we had made in February. Everything was green now, though, and it was warm. We crossed over the ice-free Charles, passed the river houses where the upperclassmen lived, and drove down into Harvard Square. I had only been to Harvard Square that once in February, but I could have been blindfolded this time when we arrived and still known exactly where we were. The energy and excitement were palpable. There was noise, but it wasn't big city noise. People ambled along the sidewalks looking in shop windows; others sat talking in outdoor cafés. I tried to imagine their conversations. Were they talking Tolstoy, politics, or baseball? I hoped all three were a possibility. There were so many people, all kinds of people. There were roller skaters and joggers, people with briefcases and kids with backpacks. The coats, wool hats, and boots that we had seen in February had been replaced with shorts, T-shirts, and sandals. I tried to take as much in as I could as we drove passed. We pulled up to Johnston Gate, the main entrance to Harvard Yard, and we filed in behind a line of cars that were waiting to get in.

"We're here, Brookie-Love," my father said. "How do you feel?"

"I'm excited but a little scared," I said.

"How about you, hon?" he said to my mother.

"The same," she said.

"Brooke Ellison for Thayer Hall," my father said to the security guard directing the cars as they pulled in.

"Turn right and follow the road all the way around the yard and it's the last building on the left, across from the church," he said.

We drove slowly past Harvard Hall, up toward Widener Library, past Weld Hall, where John F. Kennedy spent his freshman year, and down toward the church. Memorial Church, which had been dedicated to the veterans of World War I, sat right in the middle of Old Harvard Yard. Its steeple, painted a bright white, rose high above everything else, and seemed to pierce right through the blue afternoon sky. There was a golden angel at the top that appeared to watch over everything that was going on below. The ramped entrance to Thayer Hall faced the steps that led into the church. We pulled up and we parked.

"I just pakked my cah in Havid yad," my father said, opening the doors to the van and unfolding the lift so I could get out. "I always wanted to say that," he said.

As much as I didn't want to laugh, I did. I think more out of nervousness than anything else. My father was pleased to see me smile, though, because he knew that I was scared.

Thayer Hall was a five-story old redbrick building with a basement and big green wooden doors on each of its four sides. It was the home of e. e. cummings when he was a freshman and that thought gave me a rush of excitement when I drove up the ramp and maneuvered my way over the bump in through the front door. It was the same feeling that I had had on my first day back to school in the eighth grade. But this time it was on a much grander scale.

I took a few moments to allow my senses to experience my new surroundings. The walls in the hallway were beige plaster with green-painted vertical slats of wood running halfway up toward the ceiling. They smelled of fresh paint. It was a clean look and a clean smell. I could feel the history in the building and I knew how lucky I was to be a part of it. Our room was on the second floor and we took the elevator up one flight and arrived face-to-face with the crimson door of my new home: Room 212, Thayer Hall. The name tag on the door said: Brooke and Jean Ellison.

"Wait," my father said before we went in. "I didn't tell you this, but when Matt and I were up here . . . Never mind, let's just go in."

"What?" I asked.

"Nothing," my father said. "I'll tell you after we go in."

My mother turned the key, opened the door, and I couldn't believe what I saw. The room was just as I had imagined it.

We entered into a common room with high ceilings and hardwood floors. On the wall opposite the entrance door were two ceiling-to-floor windows that overlooked Harvard Yard. The green moldings accented the ivory walls, and both had been freshly painted. To the left, in the back of the room next to the windows, was a door that led to a wheelchair-accessible bathroom. The bathroom had always been there, but previous access had always been from the hallway. Brick and plaster walls had to be cut to make a new doorway that led directly into my room. To the right, about midway down the wall, was the door that led to my bedroom. It was a small room, and under the window was an adjustable bed similar to the one I had at home. There was a closet on the back wall opposite my bed and a heavy oak dresser next to the doorway. Directly off my room was the doorway that led to my mother's room. It was even smaller than mine and had a desk under the window, a dresser on the opposite wall, a closet and a regular bed along the wall next to the doorway. Most of the boxes and equipment my father and Matt had brought up were stored in the two bedrooms.

I pulled my wheelchair up to the windows and looked out into the Yard. I thought of all the people who might have looked out these windows in all the years before me. I hoped that I could live up to their standards. I could see other new freshmen unpacking their cars and wondered if any of them were as nervous as I was. Some, who had obviously gotten there earlier, were already tracking down Frisbees and tossing footballs. I wondered who, if any of them, would become my friends. There were pathways that crisscrossed the Yard and led to the exits out into Harvard Square. I could see Johnston Gate from my room and cars were still filing in. There were stately oak and maple trees that stood guard along the pathways, and one beautiful maple sat in full view just outside my window.

"Thank you," I said to the tree, whose leaves were shading the people below. "You're one friend I know I already have."

My father walked up beside me and I asked him what it was that he wanted to tell us when we got inside.

"Oh, I don't know," he said, running his hand along the molding of the window, examining the work that had been done. "I guess I just wanted to say how proud I am of both of you. You know that you are about to do something that has never been done here before," my father said. "Not in the over four-hundred-year existence of this renowned institution has anyone done what you two are about to do. No matter what happens from this moment forward, I want you both to know how proud I am of you."

He started to get that watery-eyed look that he always gets when he starts talking like that.

"I love you guys," he said.

"I love you, too, Dad. It's going to be all right," I said to him. "It's going to be all right."

JEAN

DEBBY AND I SPENT the remainder of the day unpacking boxes and organizing the bedrooms and the bathroom. Ed was with Brooke in the common room unpacking equipment and putting together furniture.

"Where do you want the futon?" he shouted after he had finished banging it together.

"Under the windows, off to the right, against the wall," I shouted back from Brooke's bedroom.

Ed looked at Brooke, she nodded her approval, and he pushed it in place.

"Let's do this now," he said, putting the assembly instructions to the computer table on a music stand in front of her.

Whenever Ed had a project to do that came with directions, he would always ask Brooke to read them to him and explain what needed to be done. It got her involved and enabled her to contribute. He knew that she needed to be a part of the activity and had to stay busy. He opened the directions to page one and asked her to get started.

"*Una el estante figo al cosado derecho,*" Brooke said to him in a Spanish accent.

"What, Brookie-Love?" Ed said.

"Oh, I'm sorry. *Attacher les tablettes fixes au panneau lateral droit,*" she said, sounding like Leslie Caron.

"Excuse me?" he said again.

"*Das feste Regal an der rechten Seitenwand befestigen,*" she said, barking orders like a German sergeant.

"What the heck are you talking about?" he said.

"We're at Harvard, Dad," she said. "I thought it appropriate that I give you the instructions in three different languages."

"Since when can you do that?" he said with an incredulous look on his face.

"Since right now," she said, laughing. "Where did we get this table from? The directions are written in every language but English. Don't worry, I'll be able to figure them out," she said smugly. "Attach the fixed shelf to the right side panel, using the fastener nuts and fastener bolts," she said.

They put the table together and set up Brooke's computer against the wall next to the bathroom door. To the left of the entrance door, they put a coffeemaker and toaster in a cabinet filled with canned foods and cereal. Off to the right, next to the coat closet, was a reading chair for me to sit in. After Debby and I were finished in the bedrooms, Ed set up Brooke's bedside ventilator and other medical equipment in a rolling cabinet next to her bed. He checked all of her battery backup systems to make sure they were working, and with all of us contributing, we were able to get most everything done that day. We all took a needed break.

Ed and I were on the futon and Debby was sitting in the reading chair. Brooke was sitting on the other side of the room looking out the window into the Yard. She had that yearning look on her face that I had seen a thousand times before. I knew what she was thinking. She wanted to get out of that chair, and there was nothing she could do about it. Ed and I looked at each other and I shook my head and sighed. There was nothing any of us could do to change that.

"Do you believe these stupid computer table instructions?" Ed said, opening up a book that he had picked up from the floor and breaking the silence in the room.

"Look, they're in every language except English," he said, smacking one of the pages in the middle of the book.

"Prepare keyboard shelf," I said, reading the first line of bold print that was in English.

"What?" Ed said, looking over at Brooke, realizing that she had caught him in a scam.

"It was more fun that way, wasn't it, Dad," she said sheepishly, but delighted that she had pulled this one over on him.

We all laughed and that just seemed to be the way our lives were. I would be ready to cry and find myself laughing. No matter what was going on in our lives, what we were doing or thinking, we could always find a reason to laugh, and that was good. I knew, though, that Ed was going to be leaving in the morning and all of the responsibility was going to fall on me. I wondered whether I had the strength to do my part and whether Brooke had the courage to do hers. I hoped, though, that no matter what we faced in the days ahead, we would both find reasons to laugh.

IT WAS A CLOUDY SUNDAY MORNING when my father and Debby left to go back to New York. They had two o'clock reservations on the Cross Sound Ferry leaving out of New London. It was a two-hour drive to get there, so they left at eleven-thirty to allow enough time for boarding.

"Just say the word if you need me, and I'll be right back up here," my father said to my mother when he hugged her and kissed her good-bye. He grabbed my arms and wrapped them around his neck. I was always his huggy bear and I missed being able to give him the hugs that I knew he loved to get. He pressed his cheek next to mine and whispered in my ear, "If you're unhappy and want to come home, just call me and I'll come get you," he said.

I knew that wouldn't happen, but I nodded my head in silence. He got in the van and drove off. My mother and I just stayed there until the van was no longer in sight. Neither one of us could stop crying and my mother was wiping my eyes and blowing her nose.

"Make sure you don't forget which tissue is yours and which one's mine," I said. "That's all I'd need right now."

My mother burst out laughing and so did I. It felt good to laugh, and so good to see her laugh, too.

"I wish we could go to the special service in Memorial Church for the incoming freshmen," I said. "I think that would make us both feel a lot better."

"Me too," my mother said. "There're just too many stairs, and you couldn't even fit a Barbie doll in the elevator they have in there. I do know that I don't want to go back to that empty room, so let's do something else."

The sun was beginning to come out, so we decided to walk around Harvard Yard. We were like a couple of grade schoolers on their first field trip to a museum. Wide-eyed with wonder, we were awestruck by Harvard's history and its grandeur.

We walked along the pathways that crossed the Yard, weaving our way around the buildings. There was a huge quadrangle of green grass that was the heart of the Yard. It was called Tercentenary Theater and was the home of so many memorable speeches and the annual Harvard graduation. It was sheltered by rows of ancient oak trees. Tercentenary Theater was surrounded by beautiful buildings of all shapes, sizes, and colors. Most of the buildings, though, were a deep red brick and looked like British estates. It was this area that separated Memorial Church from Widener Library. Widener was a huge building with a flight of stairs that seemed to go on forever. They led to a pillared entrance that could have been the gates to Heaven. I had heard that if Harvard lined up all the books that it had on campus, they would stretch for fifty thousand miles. From the size of Widener, it seemed that they all could have been in there. I learned that it was built with the money donated from Mrs. Widener, the mother of a young man who died on the *Titanic*. It was built with two stipulations. The first was that all students who attended Harvard had to have swimming lessons, and the second was that ice cream had to be served with every meal. The second stipulation I had no problem with, but teaching me to swim, I thought, was a challenge I would love to see Harvard overcome.

We walked around and saw some of the classroom buildings: Sever Hall, Emerson Hall, and Robinson Hall. I looked at my mother and she seemed to be off in another world.

"There's so much history here, Mom," I said. "They go back as far as the sixties," I said, trying to get her attention. "Did you know that Sever Hall was named after Tom Seaver, the Mets pitcher after they won the World Series back in 1969. Robinson Hall was name after Brooks Robinson because they felt sorry for Baltimore when they lost to the Mets that year, and Emerson Hall was named after the sixties rock group. I think there's a Lake Hall and Palmer Hall somewhere on campus, too," I said.

"No kidding, honey," my mother said, obviously not having paid any attention to anything that I just said.

"I think we need to get something to eat, Mom," I said, knowing that there's nothing better than food when you're singing the blues. "Let's go over to Annenberg and see what they have on the menu."

Annenberg was the freshman dining hall, but it was like no other dining hall that I had ever seen. It was almost too beautiful to eat in. Annenberg Hall looked like a Gothic cathedral from the outside. It had an enormous stained-glass rose window in the front that could compete with many of those you would find in the finest churches in Europe. Inside, it was even more majestic. The walls were covered in a deep rich wood, and halfway up, about a stretched arm's length from the floor, was a shelf that spanned the perimeter of the dining area. On the shelf, spaced about three feet apart, were busts of some of the historical figures who had attended Harvard: William Francis Bartlett, W.E.B. DuBois, Robert Gould Shaw, and the list went on and on; it was enough to make any incoming freshman feel inadequate and question why they were accepted for admission.

Behind the dining area was Memorial Hall, an area dedicated to Harvard students who were killed in the Civil War. Plaques on the walls listed the name, the Harvard class, and the date that each soldier died: 1860 Edgar Marshall Newcomb, 20 December 1862 Fredricksburg; 1861 Darden Almy, 30 August 1862 Bull Run. There was a presence in that room that made me feel connected to that time. It was as if I had been there, knew those men, and felt the loss of their passing.

Despite the therapeutic value of a good meal, we weren't able to eat very much. We each had a bagel and I learned my first lesson as a Harvard student. Bagels in Boston aren't bagels. They're round rolls with a soft crust and a hole in the middle. I wondered how long we would be able to survive without New York bagels.

On the way back from Annenberg, through the gate that led to Thayer, we could see that the Sunday freshman service had just let out from Memorial Church. There was a crowd of kids standing outside eating refreshments. The pastor was greeting members of the freshman class outside on the plaza. I decided to introduce myself and present the problem of the church's inaccessibility to the reverend.

"Good morning, Reverend. My name is Brooke Ellison and I am a first-year freshman, and this is my mother, Jean."

"It's so nice to meet you, Brooke, I'm Reverend Gomes," he said as if he were still preaching from the pulpit. "And Mom, it's so nice to meet you, too."

Reverend Gomes was a short, stout African American man who was enchanting to watch and listen to. He sounded British but I knew he wasn't. It was his eloquence, and when he spoke, he made you feel as if everything was wonderful and beautiful and there was nothing in this world that anyone needed to be concerned about. I felt at ease with him.

"I don't want to start trouble on my first day, but . . ." I went on to explain the problem that I had trying to get into the church and that I had to miss the freshman service.

"That's appalling," he said, and immediately saw the absurdity of my living only twenty feet from the church yet not being able to get in. "We'll have to see what we can do to rectify this situation," he said as if he had already taken care of it.

"You're going to stay and listen to President Rudenstine out here on the lawn, I hope. He'll be speaking in a few minutes and I know the Yard is accessible," he said with a smile.

It appeared that a good portion of the new freshman class had already assembled and I thought it would be a good idea to go over and maybe meet some of them. As I rolled along with my mother toward the crowd, I felt as though everyone's eyes were riveted on me. I had been in my wheelchair for six years and I had become used to people staring at me. I understood that there was a curiosity, and that many times people didn't even realize they were staring. For some reason, this time it felt different. I felt uncomfortable, like I was sitting there in my underwear. I wanted to scream out and say: "I was hit by a car when I was eleven years old. I'm on a respirator and, yes, this is my mother. I'm not sick and I'm not contagious." I felt my face flush as I pulled up with my mother at the edge of the crowd. People were still staring, and my mother was stroking my cheek with the back of her hand.

A girl came out from the crowd and walked over to me. "I think you could use this," she said, and took a rose that someone had obviously given to her and laid it on my lap. She rubbed my hand, smiled, and walked away. I looked at the rose and at my mother, and when I looked back at the crowd they had all turned away and were now staring at President Rudenstine.

WE HAD BEEN OUT for quite some time and Brooke was beginning to feel uncomfortable. We needed to get back to the room to take care of some of her personal needs. She drinks water all day long and needed to be catheterized, and her lungs needed to be suctioned because she was having some difficulty breathing. It was a ritual that both of us had become used to. It's just like anyone else going to the bathroom or clearing their throat, but with Brooke it takes much longer and it's a lot more difficult. I sat and rested on the futon while Brooke looked out the window at the people in the Yard. I heard footsteps on the stairs and someone was whistling.

"That sounds just like Daddy," I said to Brooke as she started to turn her chair toward the door to listen.

"It does, Mom. Do you think . . ."

The footsteps and whistling got louder and ended with a knock at our door.

"It is Daddy!" I shouted, jumping up to answer the door.

"Hi, it's me again. I just wanted to make sure you both were all right."

It was Noah, Brooke's freshman proctor, whom we had met briefly when we first arrived. He had graduated two years earlier with a degree in literature and had decided to stay on at Harvard and work with the incoming freshmen. He had applied to law school, but hadn't heard anything yet. Noah was a very gentle young man, quiet but self-assured. I think it was his maturity that got him assigned to watch over us. He was about five feet ten inches tall and had short brown hair that was just long enough to comb straight down. It was like a shorter version of what the Beatles wore back in the early sixties. The goatee that he had grown didn't quite fit his baby face.

"I just wanted to let both of you know about the proctor group meeting that we're having tonight at ten o'clock. It will be held in one of the meeting rooms next door in Canaday Hall."

Canaday was the newest of the freshman dorm buildings. It was built in 1971 and its architecture didn't really fit in with the other buildings in the Yard. It had been labeled "the projects" by the kids who were assigned there. Brooke told me that she felt bad about that because she knew a little something about what it felt like not to blend in.

"Ten o'clock P.M.?" I said to Noah, kind of surprised.

"Is that too late for you, Mrs. Ellison?" he said, a little bit concerned.

Brooke shot me a look with a message that it didn't take a genius to figure out.

"Oh no," I said. "Brooke and I are just getting warmed up at ten o'clock, and please call me Jean," I told him.

The fact of the matter was, however, that we were usually in bed by that time. Brooke and I get up very early because it takes so long to get her ready in the morning. As much as she would like to stay up late, she can't because she runs the risk of developing sores on her skin.

"That's good," Noah said. "Nothing around here ever really gets started before then, so you'll be in great shape."

Early in the evening, Ed called to tell us that he had gotten home all right and we got to speak to Kysten and Reed.

"It's very strange here without you two," Ed said. "I don't know if I'm ever going to get used to this."

"Me too," I said. "I can't tell you how many times I've turned around to call and ask you something, thinking you were there before realizing that you weren't. I miss you, sweetheart," I said.

"I miss you, too," he said.

After we got off the phone, ten o'clock couldn't come along fast enough for me because I could barely keep my eyes open. "Right about now, I should be getting under the covers," I thought to myself. Instead, Brooke and I walked over to Canaday Hall for the proctor meeting. We were the first ones to show up and I could tell that Brooke was nervous.

"Are you okay?" I asked her. "You should be used to this kind of stuff. You've been in these situations a hundred times before."

"Yeah, I know, but everybody always knew me before, or at least knew what happened to me. Nobody here knows anything about me," she said, "and I wonder what everyone's going to think."

"They'll probably be wondering what I'm doing here and won't even notice you," I said, realizing after I said it that I was probably only complicating matters by admitting that.

"I know," Brooke said. "I'm worried about that, too."

Noah came in carrying bags of chips and cookies, and it was nice to see a familiar face. He asked how we were doing and said that this was a "get to know you" meeting and would start with a preliminary explanation of rules, regulations, and expectations. Some of the kids started to trickle in, and by the time Noah was ready to get started, there were about twenty students in the room. After Noah had spoken for a while, he went around the room and asked all of us to introduce ourselves, giving our names, hometowns, and reasons for attending Harvard. When it came time for Brooke to speak, Noah asked me if I would introduce myself first. In the five years that I had been going to school with Brooke, this was the first time I had ever been included in one of these things. I was a little surprised.

"Hello everyone, my name's Jean and I'm Brooke's mother and I'm her roommate."

The expressions on the faces of the kids after I said that were very interesting. There were curious looks from everyone. One fellow pulled his glasses farther down on his nose to get a better look at us; others just kind of cocked their heads to the side, looking a little bewildered. It took a few moments for it to settle in, but ultimately it did. Inquisitive glances turned to nods of understanding and finally to welcoming smiles. I had broken the ice for Brooke and she seemed much more relaxed.

We met kids from all over the country and all over the world. It was fascinating, and everyone was so different and had a unique story to tell. Brooke became friends with Tim and Josh, who were roommates. They had both taken a year off to travel before coming to Harvard and they lived in the room on the first floor next to the entrance door to Thayer. She spoke at length with Carey, a boy from the Midwest who was terribly homesick. I think he needed to be near anything that resembled family because he missed his so much and the open spaces of his hometown.

It was a nice night and it was the first opportunity for Brooke to meet anyone. She was pleased. It was well past midnight when we got back to the room and it was the first time that I would be getting Brooke back to bed by myself. I had practiced at home and had done it when Ed and Debby were still here the night before, but this time I was completely on my own. It was scary, but I did it, and when all was said and done, I didn't get into bed until after two.

"Is the ventilator alarm on, Mom?" Brooke called to me after I had gotten into bed.

"Yes, Brooke."

"Is the intercom next to your bed?" she asked.

"Yes," I said again.

"How do you feel?" she asked me.

"I don't know if it was the coffee that I had at the meeting or what, but I'm wide awake," I said.

"You're just a party animal, Ma," she said sarcastically.

"Maybe I'll get used to this late-night stuff," I said, pulling the covers up to my chin. I lay there, stared at the ceiling, and listened to the wush of Brooke's ventilator until I fell asleep.

BROOKE

"LOOK AT ALL THE ACTIVITIES you can go to this week, Brooke," my mother said after reading a notice that had been put in the basket on our door.

"There's a mixer, an ice cream social, a barbecue, and there's even a showing of the movie *Love Story*. It says that it's a tradition here. They play it for the incoming freshmen and the outgoing seniors. I think the audience participates like they do with *The Rocky Horror Picture Show*."

Noah had distributed a list of the special Freshman Week events to all the students for whom he was proctor. I couldn't possibly go to all of them.

"What do you think you want to do today, Brooke?" she said, pulling my hair back into a ponytail and tying it off with a scrunchee.

"I can't decide, there're so many things to choose from," I said. "Let's take the list over to the dining hall. We can make up our minds while we eat."

After we passed through the gate leading to the Science Center and Annenberg Dining Hall, I realized that I couldn't stop or steer my chair.

"Where are you going, Brooke!" my mother shouted when she saw me going left toward the Science Center instead of right toward Annenberg.

I control my wheelchair with my tongue, using a retainer-like device that sits on the roof of my mouth. I was frantically hitting the buttons to try and stop or steer the chair, so I couldn't answer her. I kept driving toward the rock sculpture fountain outside the Science Center and I couldn't stop. By the time my mother realized I was in trouble, it was too late. I crashed head-on into one of the rocks in the fountain and my chair stopped dead. If I hadn't had my seat belt on, I would have been tossed into the fountain.

"Are you all right, Brooke?" my mother shouted, running over to me.

I didn't say a word; I wasn't hurt, just mortified. We were at a very busy pedestrian intersection connecting the dining hall and the Science Center to the Yard. There were students all over the place, some walking and some just relaxing by the fountain. Some kids ran over to see if I was okay, but it was one of those embarrassing situations where people realize that you're all right and just don't want to do anything that will call any more attention to the situation. They just kind of watched to see what was going to happen next.

I could turn on the power to my chair, but I couldn't get it to move. This was the first time I had any trouble with it, because it was new. I had just gotten it in May before my high school graduation. I knew we had a problem on our hands because the chair, with the batteries and ventilator on it, and me in it, weighed over five hundred pounds.

"I can't move my chair, Mom. It won't go," I said.

"Then I'll push you," she said.

My mother struggled to free my chair and managed to turn me around. A young guy came over and offered to give us a hand.

"Hi, I'm Joe, let me help you with that," he said.

"Thank you so much," my mother said. "We're going over to Thayer and I don't think I can do this myself, especially getting up that ramp and in the door. This is my daughter, Brooke, and she's a new freshman and I'm her mother, Jean. We're from Long Island," she said.

"It's nice to meet you, I'm also a new freshman and I have a room in Mass Hall. That's the building with President Rudenstine's office on the first floor. I'm okay with that, but a lot of the kids I live with feel that it cramps their style," he said. "I come from an island, too. Deer Island, it's off the coast of Maine."

I only got to see Joe briefly when he initially walked over to us. He was walking behind me, pushing my chair with my mother the rest of the way. My first thought when I saw him, though, was that he was going to hurt himself if he tried to push my chair. A lineman from the football team would have had trouble with this, I thought. What I did see was a short, slightly built young man with dark hair, but it wasn't Joe's physical appearance that told me what he was all about. It was his soft voice, his easy manner, and his genuine concern. Sometimes, in situations like this, people do things because they want to be a hero. I didn't get that feeling from Joe. He just wanted to help.

My mother and Joe pushed me up the ramp, into the building, and onto the elevator.

"Thank you so much, Joe," I said. "We couldn't have done this without you."

There was a pause, one created by his discomfort in taking credit for doing what he had just done.

"Do you want me to come up and help you get into your room?" he said.

"Oh, no thank you, Joe, you've done enough," I said, more than a little bit embarrassed by the whole situation. "I hope to see you around campus under better circumstances next time."

"Me too, Brooke, good luck," he said, and the doors to the elevator closed behind us.

We got back into our room and my mother pushed me to the middle of the floor in the common room.

"It was good that Joe came along when he did," my mother said.

"That's been happening to us ever since my accident, Ma. There's always been somebody there when we've been in trouble," I said. "These aren't coincidences."

"What are we going to do now?" my mother asked.

"I'd make a really good planter here," I said, trying to be funny, even though I was really upset.

My mother laughed, but I could see the concern on her face.

We were stuck and couldn't go anywhere. It was Freshman Week and there were a thousand things to do, and it looked like I wasn't going to be able to do any of them.

THE PHONE RANG at about ten-thirty in the morning.

"Hi, Ma, it's me. How's everything going up there?"

It was Kysten, and this was the first time she had called since we arrived up at Harvard. I had spoken to her a few times when I was on the phone with Ed, but she had never called on her own.

"Hi, sweetheart, how are you?" I said, kind of surprised to hear from her and so early in the morning.

"I'm okay, but Dad's been telling me about all the trouble you've been having up there. I feel bad that I haven't called. Is everything all right?"

"We're better now, but it's been one heck of a week," I said.

Freshman Week was over and we had spent all of it in our room. Ed, after a week of phone calls and running around, was able to get, with the help of the freshman dean's office, a company to come to the campus to fix the chair. It was running—not one hundred percent, but it was running.

"Dad said you were stuck in your room. What did you eat?"

"Thank God for Michele," I told her. "She's been bringing in food and we've been eating cereal and soup because we can't take anything out of Annenberg."

Michele was the only other nurse, aside from Debby, that we had in New York. She was looking for a change in her life, so she decided to move up to Boston when we came up to Harvard. She was coming to the room to help out until she could find a permanent year-round position somewhere else.

"You must have been going nuts. What did you do for fun all week?"

"There wasn't much we could do. We talked, read, and listened to music, but we mostly talked," I said.

"You have that little TV you brought up with you, couldn't you watch television?"

"Not really, we can't get many channels in our room and the ones we do get show mostly violence and dysfunctional people," I said. "We get a little news but it's Boston news. I really don't know what's going on down in New York."

"You're not missing much," Kysten said, "nothing's really changed, but, Ma . . ." She stopped in mid-sentence.

"What, honey?" I said.

"Do you think . . . I'm dysfunctional?"

"No, what makes you say that?" I said, taken by surprise.

"You know, with what happened after Brooke's accident. How depressed I got. I didn't want to eat, didn't go back to dancing school. I couldn't even go visit her in rehab. It's been six years and I'm still sad about it."

"We were all depressed, honey, and you were with your father at the scene of the accident. You saw your sister in the road. I thank God I was spared that. I don't know how I would have been if I saw what you saw. What happened to Brooke had an effect on everyone in the family, and I mean everyone. Your grandparents, your aunts and uncles, even your cousins. It's changed all of our lives. There still isn't a day that goes by that your father and I don't cry. Not one. But there also isn't a day that goes by when we don't laugh, either. That's what we need to focus on—the good things."

"I haven't been all that much help to you and I even gave you a hard time about going up to Harvard. I feel bad about that, too."

"Don't," I said. "I haven't been able to give you or your

brother the amount of attention that I would have wanted, and that has always upset me. It doesn't mean that I love either of you any less. It was circumstances, terrible circumstances, and I tried to spread myself around as best I could. I knew you were upset that I left again and so was I, but I couldn't have left if I thought it was something you couldn't handle. I used to really worry about you, but look at how far you've come. You're starting your junior year of college, you're holding down two jobs, you're strong and you're healthy. You've got the world on a string. I just wish you could take life less seriously and enjoy yourself more. I'm so proud of you."

"Even if I didn't go to an Ivy League college?" she asked.

"What does that have to do with anything that's real?" I said. "In the total scheme of things, it's meaningless. Brooke's coming up here was right for her. After she lost the use of her body, she had to develop her mind, and she needed the physical help that I could give her to do that. Going away to school wasn't right for you. And you have so many other interests. You got your black belt in karate, you do your athletic workouts, and you have your interests in physical health and holistic medicine. Everybody's different, and I thank God that you can do all those things. And since when does going to an Ivy League school determine a person's worth? That's a lot of nonsense."

"Do you really feel that way, Mom?"

"You know that I do. I love you so much and I love you just the way you are."

"Thanks, Mom, I hope so. I love you, too."

Kysten and I got off the phone and even though we'd had hundreds of conversations before, this one felt different. I knew how she felt and I think she understood what I was trying to tell her. It was ironic, I was much farther away from Kysten geographically, but felt much closer to her. What is it that they say about absence or distance making the heart grow fonder? Sometimes we see things much more clearly from a distance than we do when we're standing right on top of them. Kysten called every morning after that to check in, to give us the news from New York, and to tell us that she loved us.

IT WAS "SHOPPING WEEK," a unique tradition at Harvard that takes place the week before the official start of classes. It's a time during which students can attend any classes that look even remotely interesting before actually registering for them. Students can "shop" as many classes as they like, sometimes switching from one class to another every ten minutes. During shopping week students officially decide on their classes based on what they think of the professor, the course syllabus, and what they think they'll learn from the course. Professors have grown used to this concept and to the fact that during this period students walk in and out of their classrooms while their lectures are still in progress.

During the summer, I was asked by the student disability office to try to pick out the classes I wanted to take from the course catalog. They wanted me to do this early so they could move my classes to accessible locations so that I would be able to take them. I was impressed and a little embarrassed by their willingness to do that for me, but at the same time felt that they were really only treating the symptoms and not dealing with the problem.

"Why not make all the buildings accessible so they wouldn't have to disrupt anything?" I thought.

I did pick out all of my courses, so shopping week was really the first week of official classes for me. I decided on: elementary Italian; expository writing; the mandatory freshman writing course; evolutionary biology, taught by the world-renowned Nobel Prize–winning evolutionary biologist E. O. Wilson; and a literature course on the hero in Greek mythology.

Every morning, when my mother is getting me ready to face the day, we do most of our talking. We plan out what we need to do, discuss the agenda for the day, and of course, since we arrived at Harvard, pick out from the daily menu what we're going to eat at the dining hall. This was something we started way back when we were in rehab. When we lived there together, though, the circumstances were obviously dramatically different and I was only twelve years old at the time. The conversations we had back then were more mother to daughter. She spoke and I listened. Of course, she always listened to what I had to say, but I knew that if any decisions had to be made, she was going to make them. Over the past few years, especially toward the end of high school, I began to sense a metamorphosis in our relationship. She began to step back more to give me an opportunity to grow. I knew that much of what I was doing I couldn't do without her, but she deferred to me on many of the decisions that we had to make.

Since we arrived at Harvard and certainly after having been sequestered in our dorm room for a week, we really had an opportunity to talk. We talked about everything, but in a way that was different from what I had experienced before. We talked like friends. We were roommates and we discussed how each of us felt about being at Harvard. We talked about what we thought was exciting and the things that frightened us. We were open and honest and we both knew that we were in this together.

"You're the brains and I'm the brawn," my mother said to me. "Together we will overcome."

I realized that we had become two equal individual parts that, when put together, made the whole much stronger.

The conversation on the morning of the first day of classes focused primarily on what we thought my courses were going to be like. Neither one of us really knew what to expect, and so often when there's uncertainty, the imagination can wreak havoc on one's psyche. The stereotypical movie portrayals of Harvard, its students, and its professors, we thought, had never been particularly flattering. Students were usually portrayed as privileged, snobby, and stuck up. The professors were always portrayed as arrogant, stuffy tyrants who only knew how to use intimidation to motivate their students. Images of John Houseman in the movie *The Paper Chase* and Gore Vidal in *With Honors* kept running across our minds. The competitive nature of the kids I went to high school with, I thought, would pale in comparison to the students I would find at Harvard. Even though the few people I had met prior to my chair breaking down were great, I thought I wouldn't find out what Harvard was really like until I actually got into the classroom.

I was scared, unsure of myself, and maybe I was being a little unfair. Even though I expected to encounter what I had been set up in fiction to believe as true, maybe I was just as guilty in establishing uninformed prejudices in my views about Harvard, as I thought so many other people had done in forming their opinions about me.

THE LIMITED OPPORTUNITIES that Brooke had to meet people during our first week at Harvard changed dramatically once classes started. Brooke's first class was elementary Italian, which was scheduled every day, Monday through Friday, and it started at nine o'clock in the morning. We had to be up at 5:00 A.M. to give me enough time to get Brooke ready so she could get to class on time.

When Brooke and I arrived in the class, the desks were arranged in a semicircle and were rapidly filling up. By the time the class actually started at seven minutes past the hour, the time most classes started at Harvard, there were about twenty students in the room. The students were of all ages, freshmen and upperclassmen, and had obviously come from very diverse backgrounds. The instructor, Michael Hemment, looked even less Italian than his name sounded, but had apparently come from a strong Italian household, his mother having been born and raised in Italy. When he came into the classroom he wrote "Italian 1-A" on the blackboard and then proceeded to say, "These are the last words I will speak in English." Brooke thought for sure she had made a mistake and had registered for the wrong class.

"This is supposed to be *elementary* Italian," she whispered to me.

I shrugged my shoulders and didn't know what to say. As it turned out, it was the right class, and the look on Brooke's face told me she was terrified.

"Ciao, come va?" were the first and last words the instructor said that day that Brooke and I understood. He continued to

speak in long, fluid Italian sentences and neither one of us had even a glimmer of an idea of what he was saying. Brooke thought she would never survive the class.

After the class session was over, some of the kids came over to meet us. Most everyone had been given an Italian translation to their names, but there wasn't an Italian equivalent for "Brooke." She had to use her own name, which she thought sounded pretty silly in Italian.

"Hi, Brooke, I'm Viviana."

"I'm Patricia."

"I'm Giuseppe."

Vivian was from Puerto Rico, Patricia's family was from Cuba, and Joe, who was from New Jersey, was the starting goalie for the Harvard ice hockey team.

Another young man came over to introduce himself. "*Bonjour*, Brooke, I'm Austin," he said, imitating a French accent. Austin was tall and thin and of African-American heritage.

"You and I, Brooke, are the only ones without Italian trans-lations to our names. Isn't that a kick, and me with all that Italian blood in my family."

Austin had a way about him that just made everyone laugh and feel at ease.

"Did any of you understand a word that dude was saying?" Austin asked everyone.

"I didn't," Vivian said.

"Neither did I," Patricia said.

"I sure in heck didn't," Joe said. "I thought I was the only one who didn't know what was going on in that class."

They all laughed and put each other at ease. Brooke felt so much better knowing that she wasn't alone and that everyone felt the same way she did. All the kids Brooke met in that class were wonderful, down to earth, and unassuming. Even the instructor, Michael, turned out to be a joy as well, once she was able to figure out what he was talking about.

AS HAD ALWAYS BEEN THE CASE since my accident, the people I met and became closest to were guys. Early on in my freshman year I met some guys I knew would become my friends for life. Shortly after an article had been written about my mother and me in the Harvard newspaper, *The Crimson*, I met Jon in Annenberg when my mother and I were eating dinner.

"Brooke, my name's Jon. Would it be all right if I joined you and your mother for dinner tonight?" he asked me.

Jon, whose father was Chinese and his mother Caucasian, was a little shorter than average height, had black hair, a great smile and was obviously physically fit. It wasn't his physical attributes, however, that struck me about him; it was his softness, his gentleness, and his kindness that were most noticeable. Jon was spiritual, and I immediately fell in love with his spirituality.

"Please do," I said. "My mother and I would love to have your company." My mother concurred and we made room at the table for Jon to sit down.

"I read the article in *The Crimson* about you and wanted to get to know you a little better," Jon said. "When I saw you here at the table, I thought this would be a good opportunity to do that."

"I'm so glad you did. Where are you from?" I asked him, wanting to know as much about him as he did about me.

"I'm from Thayer Hall, actually. I didn't know it until I read the article, but I live right upstairs from you."

"That's wonderful, but what I meant was, where did you come from before you came to Harvard?"

He told me that he was from Hawaii, and when he spoke of his home, he spoke with reverence. He described it with such love and affection that I was entranced. He spoke about the things that mattered in his life: his family, his friends, and his faith. He told us about his parents, his brothers, his girlfriend, Jill, and his little sister, who he so sorely missed tucking in at night. He missed his home and his family and I couldn't imagine how he was feeling, being so far away from a place that he loved so much.

Jon wanted to know all about my mother and me. He said that he was amazed that my mother had gone away to school with me and we discussed the strength of family. It was interesting, but Jon told me that people with quadriplegia were fairly common in Hawaii because of the number of diving accidents that occur there. Talking to Jon was like talking to someone I had known all my life. He seemed to have an understanding not only about me but also about my entire family and what we were going through. I knew that he and I would be friends.

I decided to take the required freshman expository writing class, commonly known as expos to everyone at Harvard, during my first semester. There were a number of different course descriptions within expos and I chose "Literature and the Self." It intrigued me because the literature dealt with understanding personal identity. It also fit very nicely into my class schedule.

I didn't know it at the time, but most freshmen dread taking expos. For me, writing and literature had become important aspects of my life and I was very excited about the class. It was a small seminar class that took place in the basement of Memorial

Hall. The first exercise we did was to go around the room, each of us giving our name and telling a little bit about ourselves. As each person went, the next person had to repeat everything the previous person had said, to ensure that we were really getting to know one another. I went last and had to remember everyone else's name and information. That's when I met Brent.

Brent sat across the table from me and smiled when I repeated his information. I was a little embarrassed because I didn't know if he was just being nice or whether I had confused him with someone else. He was good-looking, had blond hair and blue eyes, and was very clean cut. He wore a button-down oxford shirt, khaki pants, and moccasins. He looked like he just walked off the page of an L.L.Bean catalog.

After class we got to talking and I could tell right away that he wasn't from the East Coast. He had a twang in his voice that was definitely midwestern. He started talking right away about the upcoming 1996 presidential election. All those things that people say about talking politics and religion held true with Brent and me. Even though both of us enjoyed talking about politics, we both quickly realized that we were on totally opposite ends of the political spectrum. We debated our opposing perspectives but ultimately resolved to agree to disagree. Brent and I got together often to talk, discussing issues that were important to both of us, even if we did have differing opinions. We seemed to have opposing views on just about every topic we could come up with. We talked about music and sports, movies and religion. Our conversations were sometimes frustrating and most times stimulating but always lively. I couldn't convert him and he couldn't change me, but we were both determined to continue trying. Brent and I were vastly different, but it was our differences that brought us together. He and I became friends.

In my travels around campus I came across so many different people I wanted to meet. I knew they all had a story to tell and I wanted to hear every one of them. Neil and I had seen each other a few times in the Yard, and when we did, we always managed to smile at each other. I finally met him when I was on my way to Sever Hall to take my Italian class and he was on his way to take Russian. I was coming from Thayer Hall and he was coming from Stoughton Hall, the freshman dorm he was assigned to, and one morning he caught up to my mother and me and just started talking.

Neil was a muscular guy, over six feet tall, with short brown hair and a smile that stretched from ear to ear. He was on the heavyweight crew team and that, along with many other things in life, was one of his passions. Neil talked about crew like he did any other subject during the course of a conversation, with energy and excitement. When he opened his mouth, you knew he was brilliant, but there was also a goofiness to his brilliance. He was so positive and happy that, when he spoke, it was difficult to concentrate on what he was saying because he was so captivating in his delivery.

He grew up on a farm in New Hampshire with his older sister and younger brothers, and it quickly became clear that his family was one of the joys in his life. He had attended Exeter, the prestigious private school in New Hampshire, before coming to Harvard, but it was obvious that he had none of the pretentiousness that one would think you might find in a guy who came from a school like that. Everything was beautiful to Neil: he loved people, he loved God, and he loved life. Neil, like Jon and Brent, became my friend. They were so different but they became my friends, and that was the biggest reason why I knew Harvard was exactly where I was supposed to be.

FOR BROOKE AND THE REST of the freshmen, the period between the first day of classes and Thanksgiving was a long stretch
without an official break. For me, it seemed like an eternity. The
brain, though, with its built-in safety mechanisms, prevented me
from clearly remembering finite units of time. Each day passed
by very slowly, but when I looked back on them, the weeks
seemed to go by very quickly. Ed had been beating a path from
our home in Stony Brook to Cambridge, as he would try to visit
us as often as he could. Always with a smile on his face and never
with any questions, Ed would do supply runs and visit on weekends. Reed would come up with him as much as he could, but
it was his biggest year in high school and he often couldn't get
away. Kysten, who was going to school and working, hadn't come
up to visit at all, and even though I spoke to her at length on the
phone every morning, I missed seeing her. I missed her, I missed
Reed, and I missed Ed. I missed being in my own home, seeing
my friends, and the time I used to get to myself when Ed or
Debby would relieve me.

There was never a time that Brooke and I weren't together.
We could be in separate rooms, but I could never be in a place
where I couldn't hear her. I couldn't just go for a walk, run to
the store, or even go out in the hall without fear of locking the
door behind me. I showered with the bathroom door open and
I slept with a room monitor next to my ear. It was twenty-four
hours a day, seven days a week. It was what I did, but I never
viewed it as my "job." No one would ever take a job like that. A
labor of love doesn't come with a job description, a contract, or

a bargaining agreement. It is something that is done from the heart without thought of compensation. As difficult and as exhausting as it was, what I was doing brought joy into my life. I didn't see it as a sacrifice and I wasn't becoming a martyr. If I felt that way, I would have grown resentful, and that most certainly would have brought disaster.

Brooke was making friends, mostly guys, and they would come by often to talk and just be together. She was happiest when she was with her friends. Unlike at home, where my friends had become Brooke's friends, at Harvard, her friends had become mine. Living in a freshman dorm didn't give me too many opportunities to establish adult relationships. It was five floors of seventeen- and eighteen-year-olds who were, for the most part, getting their first real experience with freedom. The music was loud and the kids were noisy. They kept me tired, but they also kept me feeling young. When Brooke would hear a song coming from another dorm room she would often quiz me on the song title, name of the group, and the type of music. In the beginning, I failed miserably, but as time went on, I got pretty good at it. I would usually get the right answer on either the first or second try.

Living the dorm life didn't just create social problems for me, but I think it was actually more difficult for Brooke. Even though she had made some wonderful friends, friendship was as far as it ever went. It was immensely frustrating for her. Our room was right across from the elevator, and it was a natural place for kids to congregate. Going out partying late at night was something Brooke couldn't do, and hearing the comings and goings of kids all night long became a constant reminder of that fact. She saw romance everywhere she went on campus, but in the dorm it was something that stared her right in the face.

It was inexplicable to me, but I never experienced with Brooke the usual tensions that you find in a mother and daughter relationship. It was the sadness that would come over her that I would find so difficult to deal with. It was one particular Saturday night when everyone was going out and Brooke and I were staying in. She was sitting at her computer crying. I knew it was about something I had little control over and couldn't really make better. We sat and talked.

"It's so unfair, Mom. I can talk to guys about anything, but that's as far as it goes. I'm stuck in this situation and no one can really see past it."

"That's not true," I said. "You know there are guys in your life who love you."

"That's not what I mean. My 'love' life is fine, it's my . . . never mind, no one really understands."

"I understand, but no one knows what tomorrow will bring. No one can say for certain that the way things are today are the way they're going to be next week."

"It's been six years, Mom."

"You're not alone in this world. You're not the only person facing relationship problems. It's universal, and you certainly don't have to be in a wheelchair to experience it. Look around you, review the statistics, pick up any paper and look at the personal ads. It's not easy for anyone to find a relationship."

"Is that supposed to be a consolation? And anyway, that's easy for you to say. You've got Dad."

"We were just lucky, honey, I have no illusion about that. If I hadn't moved out to Long Island from Brooklyn, or if I had moved to a different town, I probably never would have met your father. Then who knows."

"You know that you two were meant to be."

"Well, if you believe that, then what happens to you is also meant to be, and you'll find your soul mate, too."

"Does everybody realize how fortunate they are? Do they really appreciate what they have and what they are able to do?"

"Do you?" I asked. "Everybody is suffering in some form or another. No one on this planet has a monopoly on pain. It's what we do with it that matters. If we all sat and focused on what we didn't have, we'd all be miserable. I'm not minimizing what you're going through, but when you start thinking like this, you need to redirect your thoughts to the good things in your life, and there are so many good things."

Brooke and I talked until we were interrupted by a knock at the door. I quickly wiped Brooke's eyes, smoothed down her hair, and answered the door. It was Jon from upstairs.

"I wasn't doing anything tonight, Brooke, so I thought if you weren't busy, you might want to see some pictures that I took of Hawaii. Maybe after that we could just hang out together and talk for a while," he said.

Brooke gave me a smile as I left the room. It was a smile of affirmation. As had been the case so many times before, someone had come through her door at a time when she most needed it. Isn't it that way with all of us, people often walk into our lives just at the right time, we just have to recognize it when it happens.

BROOKE

THE HARVARD/YALE FOOTBALL GAME was at Harvard my freshman year. It alternates from Harvard to Yale every year and, traditionally, it's the weekend before Thanksgiving. My father and brother came up the Friday before the game not only to enjoy the festivities but also to take my mother and me home for the holiday. Harvard/Yale Weekend in the fall is one of the biggest weekends of the year at Harvard. Alumni of all ages come back to the campus to watch rivalrous events not only in football but also between musical groups and drama departments. It seemed contradictory, like listening to opera between rounds of a heavyweight fight, to go watch two football teams bash their heads together in the afternoon and then in the evening watch an a cappella singing battle between the Harvard Krokodiloes and the Yale Whiffenpoofs.

"They alternate every year?" my father asked me after I told him the agenda for the weekend. "I want to come up here when the a cappella groups play football and the football players sing against each other. Now that would be fun to watch," he said with a grin, moving his eyebrows up and down as he often did when he wanted to get a rise out of me.

We all went to the big game on Saturday afternoon, and despite my father's disappointment that it was actually the football players playing, both he and my brother had a great time. I got the sense from my father's reactions to the game that he was becoming a part of Harvard life along with my mother and me. I think my mother's being there with me and the fact that he was up there so often really got him involved. He had gone to concerts and sat in on some of my professors' lectures, but what I sensed he enjoyed the most was getting to know my friends.

We all left Harvard early on Wednesday morning and made the five-and-a-half-hour trip back to Long Island the way my father always traveled: on the Cross Sound Ferry. There are a number of different ferryboats that sail across the sound, and my father prided himself on knowing the schedules of all of them.

He was on those boats so often that he was on a first-name basis with many of the crew members.

"I think we'll be taking the *Cape Henlopen* home this morning, and Derek's working on that boat," my father said, very satisfied with himself that he knew something we didn't. "And we'll be taking the *John H* back," he said, pausing for a moment. "Isn't that appropriate, the *John H* and you're going back to Harvard," he said, looking as if he had just figured out the secret to Rubik's Cube. "Get it, *John H*, John Harvard?" he said, still looking for a response from us and growing impatient.

"Yes, we get it!" we all said in unison. My father has a way of bludgeoning a point so badly that you feel like your head is going to cave in.

When we arrived home, it at first seemed strange to be there, but I adjusted quickly and could see how happy my mother was to be home. She walked around the house, absorbing all the rooms as if she were storing them away to be lived in when we got back to Harvard. We weren't home long, but as it turned out it was just long enough to eat a good meal, reunite with the family, and to learn that my grandfather didn't have much longer to live.

JEAN

NEW YEAR'S EVE, 1996, Ed's father died. It was almost as if he waited for us to get home so that the whole family could be there for each other. Brooke and I were so worried that something might happen when we weren't home, but it was just like Ed's father to accommodate us. In life he had always put his family first, so, too, in death.

After the funeral, Brooke and I went back to Harvard so she could take her exams and close out the first semester. Harvard has this annoying habit of scheduling exams after the Christmas holiday. It's their equivalent of putting coal in all the students' stockings. Brooke had to study all through the holidays. Just like she did in high school, Brooke had to take her exams separately. Short answers she had to give orally, and for essays, she needed her voice-activated computer. She was assigned a proctor to oversee her exams. Her name was Valerie. Valerie was a soft, gentle woman who was a caring soul. She not only watched over Brooke's exams but also looked after us. We became friends.

The spring semester seemed like a misnomer to us because it started in the dead of winter. As was the case with the fall semester, the spring semester began with "shopping week." By the end of their freshman year, all students were to have decided on a major, what Harvard calls a concentration, and typically a freshman's spring semester schedule was chosen to help in that decision-making process. Brooke wasn't sure what she wanted to major in, but she was leaning toward psychology and biology. She registered for an opera class, a philosophy class, a second semester of Italian, and astrophysics. Go figure.

Philosophy was never my cup of tea. It always seemed to me that philosophers just wanted to go out of their way to explain very commonsense issues in ways no one could understand. And astrophysics, even though the professor was very entertaining, I don't think I could even begin to try to explain that class. With my going to Italian with Brooke five days a week for a year, even I was beginning to pick up the language. I was finding that class to be fun and the opera course . . . what a joy that was. I listened and enjoyed arias while Brooke had to analyze them. I could have sat in that class every day of every week for the entire time we were at Harvard.

In addition to the selection of a concentration, second semester freshmen find out what upperclassman house they're going to live in for the remainder of their Harvard career. Harvard has a rather unique housing system. Incoming freshmen generally live in the buildings that are located within the protected confines of Harvard Yard. After freshman year, students are moved from their freshman dorms to one of the thirteen upperclassman houses. Under a program known as "randomization," freshmen can't choose the house they want to live in but they can join a "blocking" group of up to sixteen students who would all be assigned to a house together at the end of freshman year. Housing assignments are a big deal on campus and they are traditionally given on the last day of class before spring break.

There are two groups of upperclassman houses: the river houses and the quad houses. The river houses, as their name implies, are located along the Charles River and are very old, most having been built during the early 1900s. The river houses epitomize Harvard in their appearance. They are like colonial mansions built from red brick that house dorm rooms with fireplaces and dining halls that resemble stately libraries. For those reasons, and the fact that they are located closer to Harvard Yard where most of the classrooms are, they are usually the most desirable houses to be assigned to.

The quad houses, on the other hand, are newer in style and design, having been built in the mid- to late twentieth century, and are somewhat removed from campus. They are located about a mile north of Harvard Yard. There are three quad houses and ten river houses.

As soon as Brooke's spring semester got going, Noah; Brooke's freshman dean, Lorraine Sterritt, who had been so helpful to us during Brooke's freshman year; and the Harvard disability office wanted to make arrangements for her future housing. Even though Harvard had made extensive renovations to the freshman dorm, they wanted Brooke to move along with her class and decided that they would renovate all over again in a different location. Finding the right one, though, was going to be a project. Because of the age of the river houses, they had no elevators, and very tight quarters. As a result, virtually all of the river houses were eliminated as choices for her. For all intents and purposes, Brooke would have to be assigned to one of the three quad houses.

The quad houses were called that because all three—Pfortzheimer, Cabot, and Currier—along with Hilles Library were arranged in a square with a big grassy field in the middle. It formed a quadrangle. It was a relatively quiet and serene place compared to where we were used to living. While the rest of the Harvard campus was embedded in the busy city streets of Cambridge, the quad houses were nestled in a much more residential area north of the Square.

We first looked at Pfortzheimer House and Cabot House. As an undergraduate, Pfortzheimer had been Noah's house and he wanted us to go there; however, the elevators in both Pfortzheimer and Cabot were too small. That left only Currier House, and I could tell that Brooke was getting nervous thinking that there would be no housing available for her.

Currier House was located on Garden Street, a main thoroughfare that ran parallel to Mass. Avenue, and between Linnaean Street and Shepherd Street. It was the most modern of the three houses and looked a lot like the Canaday "projects" in Harvard Yard. It didn't have the traditional Harvard look, but it had the only look that was going to work for Brooke. We checked out some rooms, and although every one of them would require extensive renovations, we found something that we thought would work for her.

Because she knew the house she was going to be living in, Brooke couldn't block with her friends. The decision would not have been "random" for them, and they would in effect be choosing their house. This concerned her, because she didn't want to be separated and so far away from her friends. There was nothing she could really do, Currier House was the only house that could accommodate her.

B R O O K E

WE MET CARA, or rather my parents did, the first day we arrived at Currier House to start my sophomore year. I hadn't gotten out of the van yet and my mother and father were unloading some of the boxes that had been packed around me. Cara came by and offered to help.

"Hi, can I help you with something?" she asked on her way into the building.

"No, I think we'll be all right," my father said, "but that was very kind of you to offer. My name's Ed and this is my wife, Jean, and my daughter, Brooke, who's still in the van, is starting her sophomore year here. Actually, Jean will be living here with Brooke as well."

"I'm Cara, it's nice to meet you," she said. "I'm a senior here in Currier."

Cara was a tall, athletic-looking African-American woman. She had skin that looked like chiffon and a warm and engaging smile. There was an elegance about Cara; she carried with her a pride that told anyone who met her that she knew who she was and where she was going. She had obviously seen that I was in a wheelchair and asked my father what had happened to me. My father explained the situation and told her that I had sustained a spinal cord injury. Cara then told us that she had taken a year off from school and had gotten involved over the summer with nerve regeneration. She said that she was very much interested in spinal cord research and would like to talk to me after I got settled in.

We had pulled up to the Garden Street side of Currier House. The main entrance was off Linnaean Street, but Manny, the Currier House superintendent, had said that they had made arrangements for us to park on the Garden Street side of the building.

We had received a copy of the blueprints over the summer for the renovations that were being done and had been involved in some of the planning, but as Robert Burns said: "The best laid plans . . ." We really weren't sure what we would find when we got there.

They had decided to not only renovate the inside rooms, but they had obviously worked on the outside as well. They had constructed a large wooden ramp with metal railings that led to a remote-controlled entrance into the house. We were met by Manny and Patricia, the assistant to the house masters. Manny, who was Hispanic, had a goatee and dark features that reflected his heritage. He spoke with an accent that was only slightly reminiscent of his background and had almost a childlike softness about him. He was one of the most agreeable men my mother and I had ever met. His easygoing manner was only exceeded by his efficiency. We only had to suggest something to Manny and it was done.

Patricia was a short bubbly woman whose short curly brown

hair reflected her personality. She was younger than my mother but old enough for her and my mother to identify with each other. Her being from New York was also something they both had in common. Patricia was there to meet us and to see if there was anything we needed. She greeted us warmly, made us both feel welcome, and she and my mother became friends.

Manny gave my mother a remote control that she could use not only to open the doors to the building but also the doors to our new room. Our new entrance had been strictly an emergency exit that previously had no access from the outside. It was still an emergency exit but was now going to be an entrance for my mother and me. They didn't want everyone coming in and out through there because of the security problems it would create. The Harvard Shuttle was set to pick us up and drop us off at the bottom of the new ramp on Garden Street.

Even though we had seen the inside of Currier House when we visited during my freshman year, we didn't get a real good look at it. We were struck by how nice it was when we arrived that first day. Opposite our entrance doors were two doors that led to a balcony area, where there were a few administrative of-fices. This indoor balcony was in the shape of a big rectangle and looked down onto a dance floor and ballroom. They called it the Fishbowl because people could stare down into it from the bal-cony above. It was the first thing you saw when you entered the building.

When we turned right, we went down a hallway into Gilbert Tower, one of the four towers that made up Currier House, each named after a distinguished Radcliffe alumnus. Currier House had officially opened in September 1970 and was named after Audrey Bruce Currier, Class of '56, who was killed along with her husband in a plane crash in 1967. Our room, or should I say our home for the next three years, was 101 Gilbert Tower. As was the case in Thayer, our room was just past the elevator. It was convenient, but we already knew the problems associated with living near the elevator.

My mother hit the button on the remote control that Manny had given her and, with a loud buzzing sound, the oversized door to the suite swung open. It opened into a bedroom that was going to be my room. It was significantly larger than my bedroom in Thayer Hall and it had a handicapped-accessible bathroom off to the right. To the left was a doorway that led into another room, which was going to be my mother's bedroom. It was a little bit smaller than my room, but it, too, had its own bathroom. Both of these rooms had windows that looked out onto Garden Street. We could hear and see the traffic and people walking by. It was more comforting than it was noisy. Beyond my mother's bedroom was an eat-in kitchen, equipped with a refrigerator, oven, stove, sink, and cabinets. To the right, at the end of the kitchen, was a short hallway with a window on the right and another bathroom on the left. The hallway led into a living room that had windows that also looked out onto Garden Street. The suite was much more than I had ever hoped for.

"I love it," I said to my mother. "What do you think?" I asked her.

"It's going to take me all day just to keep these bathrooms clean," she said, looking around and obviously a little embarrassed by the size of the place.

I HAVE OFTEN HEARD THE EXPRESSION that the journey is its own reward. This message, like the serenity prayer, has been one that I have had to remind myself of regularly not only to sustain me in my own life but also in my efforts to help Brooke in hers.

During the summer of 1997, between Brooke's freshman and sophomore years, I felt an urgency in my life. I kept thinking that time was passing by too quickly and that all of us were just getting older. Kysten was starting her senior year in college, Reed was entering his senior year in high school, and I felt that Ed and I were rapidly approaching our senior years in life. I knew that the older we got the faster the years seemed to go by, and I knew that I would never have those years back again.

It was going to be a big year for both Reed and Kysten. They were both finishing up stages of their academic careers. Reed was finishing high school and was looking at prospective colleges while Kysten was finishing up college and looking for job opportunities. I knew there would be applications to fill out, interviews to go on, and graduation parties to plan. I wanted to be involved in all of that, spend time with them and with Ed, and still be able to take care of Brooke's needs.

In his search for potential colleges, Reed had decided that he was going to come up to Boston to go to school. He said that when he visited us up at Harvard he liked it up there, and he wanted to be close enough to be able to visit us and spend time with Brooke. He decided to apply to Harvard, Tufts, and Boston University. We all knew that Harvard would be a stretch for Reed; his SATs were excellent but his grades weren't as good as

Brooke's. The thought of his possibly coming up there and being with us made Brooke and me very excited. Even though we both were hoping he would come to Harvard, we felt that either of the others would be fine. You could hit any of those campuses with a rock if you threw one out of Harvard Yard.

Kysten wanted to do anything that involved working in the health field. She was studying health education, counseling, and nutrition. Her interests were primarily in holistic medicine and she was working in a health food store, but she had also taken a job in a chiropractor's office, had worked at the university's medical center, and was working with a local cardiology group. Her immediate plans after college were to continue working and to look for a job teaching health on the secondary level.

Ed was still working for Social Security and had been with them now for over twenty-three years. It was a job he had taken right out of college just to hold him over until he found something else. He had gotten his M.B.A. back in the seventies, but he was a true child of the sixties. He needed to have a job that he felt was socially relevant. He loved meeting and talking to people and trying to help them when they had problems. It was working in the bureaucracy that upset him. He often couldn't do as much as he wanted to help people and that frustrated him. Fortunately, for both Ed and the rest of us, his career wasn't the most important part of his life.

"It's a living, not a life," he would say when he talked about his career. Whenever anyone met him and asked him what he did, he would say, "I'm a father and I'm a husband and I work for Social Security to support that effort."

During those summer months before school started, I found myself trying to cram in as much life as I could while I was home. I felt that I needed to make the most out of the time I had while

I was there. I wanted to see everyone, do everything, and make sure the time we were spending together was "quality" time. I was trying to fill myself up, thinking that if I had a full tank when it came time to leave again in September, I could draw on that and it would sustain me when I was away. I also felt that, in some way, it would help appease any guilt I might have for not being home. I was wrong. I was trying too hard. I was trying to do too much and realized that I was just forcing my life. I hadn't learned the lesson that I was trying to teach Brooke: to enjoy life moment by moment, day by day, and to learn that happiness can only be found from within. I had to step back, let go, and savor each moment as it happened. It didn't matter what any of us were actually doing in life, it was the journey through it that was its own reward.

BROOKE

AS BEAUTIFUL AS ANNENBERG DINING HALL WAS, it was difficult to get to in bad weather or when either my mother or I was sick. My difficulties getting to and from Annenberg only further cut down on my ability to socialize. The dining halls for upperclassmen, however, are located in their respective houses. This made life so much easier for my mother and me. For us, socialization at Harvard took place the same way it did at home, over a meal. That's the way we do it at home and I think that's the way it's done in most households. A meal does more than just provide sustenance; it's considered an opportunity. It's a time to catch up with one another, to tell each other jokes, or to just talk about anything that happens to cross one's mind. The kitchen is where everything happens in our house, and I realized very quickly that the dining hall was "mission control" at Currier.

After we had gotten set up in our rooms, and my father had left and returned to New York, we made our way down to the dining hall. The dining hall was just one floor down on the elevator and was located right across from the Fishbowl. Annenberg's size and majesty were replaced by Currier's warmth and convenience. You could have dropped Currier's dining hall into the middle of Annenberg and it would have been lost. As you walked into the dining hall, there was a garden that sat right in the middle of the dining area. It was a square about ten feet by ten feet and there was a skylight of equal size in the ceiling above it. There were wooden tables that radiated out from the garden and lined up in rows around the perimeter of the room. Those tables weren't just places where you ate. It wasn't surprising to see people in their pajamas and bathrobes at them in the morning, or sitting and studying at them at night. There were always students sitting and talking, playing games, or just relaxing.

One of the nicest aspects of house living is that you don't just live with other students. There are always little kids and adults around with whom students can interact. It's like a big family. Upperclassman life is different from freshman life. Instead of freshman proctors, upperclassmen have tutors who live in the houses to oversee the students and help resolve their problems. Tutors are typically graduate students from all different disciplines who give advice, help plan courses of study, and are there to hear and address student concerns. They plan parties and study breaks, and become friends with the students they work with.

The tutors are overseen by the house senior tutor. The senior tutor lives in the house with his family, and that often includes children of all ages. The senior tutor is ultimately overseen by the house masters, Harvard professors who usually live in the houses with their families. The house masters oversee everything in the house and have overall responsibility for its operation.

We met Diane and Honey the first time we walked into the dining hall. Diane was standing at the salad bar, making sure there were enough tomatoes in the tomato bin. She was in her fifties, with blond hair and glasses, and she was wearing a Harvard dining staff uniform. When she saw my mother and me come in, she gave us a big smile and came right over to greet us.

"Well, hello there," she said in a thick Boston accent, "my name is Diane and this is Honey." She gestured for her friend to come over and meet us. "We work here in the dining hall and you'll be seeing a lot of us, I'm sure. I guess you two are new here?"

My mother and I introduced ourselves and I realized right away that a bond had been created between Diane and my mother almost immediately. There was something about the two of them that just clicked. It may have been their common heritage, both having Italian-American backgrounds. It may have been their common experience, both cared for a disabled child, or it just may have been that they were two human beings reaching out to each other, wanting to be friends.

"Has anyone shown you the ropes around here yet?" Diane asked us.

We said that we had taken a quick tour but really didn't know all the ins and outs. She proceeded to tell us how the dining hall operation worked and what we had to do when we came in, and then she introduced us to some of the other dining hall staff.

"This is Chris, our chef," she said, introducing us to a man in his early thirties wearing a white uniform, apron, and chef's hat.

The fact that Chris was a body builder was evident. I didn't think they made a chef's uniform big enough to accommodate his massive physique. He was about five feet ten inches tall, had a ruddy complexion, and shoulders that two grown men could have sat on and he probably wouldn't have known they were even there.

"Anything special you want, you just let me know," Chris said to me. "You, too, Mrs. Ellison. Just ask me and I'll fix it right up for you," he said.

Diane, Honey, and Chris were very protective. They took my mother and me under their wings and watched over us as they did all the students who came into their dining hall. They made sure everyone was happy and well fed.

JEAN

BROOKE AND I DECIDED TO GO into Harvard Square to get some of her books and to visit the Yard. We hadn't been back to either place since the end of her freshman year. Getting around this year was going to be very different from before. Thayer Hall, having been located in the Yard itself, was within walking distance of just about everything. Virtually all the classroom buildings were either in or near the Yard, and Harvard Square was located just outside Johnston Gate.

Currier House, on the other hand, was a mile north of the Square, and although we could walk it if we had to, the streets and sidewalks weren't that conducive to wheelchair travel. We were going to have to use the Harvard Shuttle Service on a regular basis. We would have to call, tell them what time to come pick us up, tell them where we were going and what time we needed to come back. It was like calling a taxi service, but instead of a cab we would get a van with a wheelchair lift in it. Harvard had made the necessary modifications to their vans by removing the seats that had created the problem for Brooke on our first visit to the school.

The van pulled up to the Garden Street entrance, and as we made our way down the ramp an older gentleman got out to get the lift ready. He had a slight build and gray hair, and was probably in his early sixties. He was really too young to be Brooke's grandfather, but from the way he handled her he could very well have been.

"You must be Brooke, it's so nice to meet you, sweetheart," he said with a thick Boston accent, and started to help her get on the lift. "My name's Bob and I'm at your service today," he said as if he were taking the Queen of England for a jaunt out of Buckingham Palace.

He and I introduced ourselves and then he went on to talk to Brooke about every topic imaginable. They broke the ice with the obligatory weather conversation and what they thought the winter was going to be like, but then went on to talk about almost everything. They talked sports: Brooke is a Mets fan; Bob, of course, roots for the Sox. They talked politics, current events, and even food.

"Do you know where we can get some good Chinese food around here?" Brooke asked him.

He did and was even able to tell us where we could get a halfway decent bagel. He and Brooke were friends immediately.

Bob dropped us off in the Square, just outside the Coop, and we made arrangements for a pickup later in the afternoon. The Coop, which is short for "Cooperative," is the Harvard bookstore. But it doesn't just sell books; it has a little bit of everything. Since Brooke and I can't get out and do much shopping, it turned out to be a godsend for us last year at Christmas. Everyone got a gift from the Coop, and I think Brooke and I may have single-handedly cleaned out their entire stock of Harvard sweatshirts.

Brooke's course load this semester was going to be a doozy. She had finally decided at the end of last year that her major was going to be cognitive neuroscience. It is a combined concentration in psychology and biology and was exactly what she was looking for. It provided a more scientific perspective on psychology by studying not only behavior but neurology, an area of great interest to her because of her spinal cord injury. The courses that she needed to get books for were organismic and evolutionary biology, statistics, early childhood development, and a sophomore tutorial class in cognitive neuroscience. The cost of just the books alone was over five hundred dollars, and there were so many that I could barely carry them out of the store.

Harvard Square looks a lot like a mini Greenwich Village with its shops, cafés, and street performers. Brooke and I decided to walk around the Square a while and look in some of the other stores. We had apparently forgotten the frustration we had had the year before. Virtually none of the stores in the Square were accessible. The few that she could actually get into only allowed her past the front door. Beyond that it's impossible to maneuver in the aisles.

"They might as well put up signs saying 'No Wheelchairs Allowed' or 'Able-Bodied People Only,' " I said to Brooke, becoming more and more angry with each store we came across that we couldn't get into.

"Calm down, Mom," Brooke said, realizing that I was about to lose it. "Let's go into the Yard and walk around for a while," she said.

We made our way through the Square and I was seething. We entered the Yard through the Johnston Gate entrance.

"Let's check out Thayer, Mom," Brooke said in a voice that was obviously intended to try and calm me down.

"All right," I said, but I was still really angry.

We crossed through the Yard and passed by the statue of John Harvard.

"I heard that that's not really John Harvard," Brooke said.

"No, who is it?" I asked her.

"Some guy named Yale," she said, trying to get me to laugh and stop thinking the thoughts she knew I was thinking.

We turned the corner around University Hall to get to Thayer and there, staring us right in the face in front of Memorial Church, was a big, beautiful wooden ramp winding its way up to the front doors. I looked at Brooke and she looked at me and, as usual, we both started to cry. It could not have come at a better time or have been in a better place. As we made our way toward the ramp we saw Reverend Gomes walking toward us, swinging his cane on his way through the Yard.

"I hope to be seeing your two beautiful faces in church on Sunday," he said, tipping his hat and walking by with a satisfied smile on his face.

"Indeed you will," Brooke said, and we made our way up the ramp and into the church. When I sat down inside, I realized that my anger was gone.

"This was no coincidence, Brooke," I said.

"I know, Mom. It's just the way life is," she said. "How do you feel now?"

"Better, sweetheart, much, much better."

BROOKE

"HELLO, IMELDA," Honey said to me as my mother and I entered the dining hall. She had taken to calling me Imelda when she realized how many different pairs of shoes I had.

"Let's see which ones you're wearing today," she said, lifting up my pant legs to take a peek.

"One day I'm going to surprise you, Honey, and I'm not going to be wearing any shoes," I told her.

"Then I'll just have to call those your clear shoes, if you do that, sweetie," she said, walking over to straighten out the salt and pepper shakers at the table where my mother and I usually sit.

My mother had gone over to talk to Diane and they were obviously having a serious conversation. I went in to see what looked good for dinner. Cara was already on line and she was with her roommate, Jen, and her friend Johnisha. Jen and Johnisha were juniors, and even though Cara was a senior, she and Jen roomed together. Cara and I had become good friends over the course of the semester, and since she knew just about everybody in the house, I got introduced to a lot of people.

My mother and I usually sat at the first table off to the left as you walk into the dining hall. It's near the desk where Diane and Honey check student ID cards and it's also a good place to be to say hello to everyone as they arrive for dinner. I wheeled myself over and got myself in the usual position at the table. My mother came over with a tray with two dinners on it and sat down to my right, as she always did.

"What's up with Diane?" I said. "Is everything all right?"

"I was just telling her about the rough night we had last night and she was telling me that she had trouble with her son, too. We were just commiserating."

She removed the device from my mouth that I use to control my chair and wrapped it in a napkin and stuck it behind my shoulder. As she strategically placed the plates down on the table so she could help both herself and me, the Grahams walked in with their son, Powell, and stopped to say hello.

"How's the food tonight?" Bill Graham asked, hoping for a positive response.

"Haven't started yet," my mother said. "But it sure smells good."

Barbara and Bill Graham are the co-masters of the house. They are husband and wife and are in their early forties. Their son, Powell, is eleven going on thirty. Barbara is associate director of the university library system and Bill is a professor of religion and Islamic studies. I think between the two of them they have more degrees than a thermometer. That might sound clichéd, but at least in their case I don't think it's hyperbole. They are both short and lean with light brown hair, and it's uncanny, but if it weren't for Bill Graham's obvious southern accent, they could easily pass for brother and sister. The fact that they are scholars is evident in their speech and appearance, but there is no arrogance or pretense associated with it. They are wonderful, gentle, helpful people who always made my mother and me feel very much at home.

"Enjoy your meal, sorry to hold you up," Barbara said as my mother tucked a napkin under my chin.

Cara, Jen, and Johnisha, who had obviously gotten hung up talking to friends on the line, came over and set their trays down. Jen is short, with brown hair and clear white skin. She is self-assured and always looks like she has just come out of the shower. She plays on the women's hockey team, and it's obvious she has a clean and healthy look.

Johnisha, whose mother is Jewish and father is African American, has skin like cream, and when her long, wavy, jet black hair lays against it, you can see that she is uniquely beautiful. Johnisha is quiet but not timid, and when she talks, it's as if she thinks someone's asleep in the room. She never speaks above a whisper.

"What do you want to start with, Brooke?" my mother said, anxious to eat before everything got cold.

"The chicken," I said, "then just work your way around the plate in a circle. Everything looks delicious."

As was usually the case when it was just girls at the table, the conversation centered on guys. I thought it was great that everyone felt comfortable enough to share those conversations with my mother. My friends had become her friends and she was just part of the group. The talk was the standard kind of banter: who everyone thought was cute, who they thought was available, all that kind of stuff. Dave, who had come over and also set down his tray, was openly gay, so no one felt the need to change the subject. My mother, in deference to my father, would usually just passively participate. She would either nod her head in agreement, make a face, or shrug her shoulders, but she would rarely voice her opinion in matters of that sort. There were times, though, when she just couldn't help herself.

"Now *he's* good-looking," my mother said emphatically, without reservation, glancing toward the entrance to the dining hall.

Everyone turned slowly to see who my mother was referring to, trying not to be too obvious.

"You mean Mike?" Cara asked, implying that all my mother had done was cite the obvious. My mother nodded, a little embarrassed for not having been able to contain her remark.

"Everybody thinks he's gorgeous," Cara said. "You're not going to get any arguments from anyone at this table."

Mike and Abraham, two senior friends of Cara's who had since become friends of mine, had come into the dining hall.

Mike was six feet six inches tall and was the captain of the fencing team. He was from Slovakia and had a body like an Adonis. His chiseled facial features and deep blue eyes were perfect under his curly light brown hair. And just like tonight, anytime he walked into a room, heads would turn. To most of the girls in the house, he was the object of their affection, but believe it or not, to me it wasn't his looks that I found most attractive. It was who he was, not what he looked like. He was caring, compassionate, and always polite, and that's what I loved about Mike.

Mike and Abraham were roommates but couldn't have been more different from each other. Abraham was rather short, with black hair and a dark complexion. He had been born in Cuba but moved with his family to Miami when he was very little. Abraham could always be found shuffling back and forth from the dining hall to the television, and he was possibly one of the smartest and funniest people I had ever met. He would come to my room and we would play Scrabble or Trivial Pursuit; we'd watch movies or just talk for hours. He was even able to teach me chess, but I was no match for him or for Mike. When they played against each other, they played like champions. I loved to spend time with both Mike and Abraham; individually and together they were always perfect company. The two of them, each with their own slight accent, could always find a way to make me laugh.

"Hey, you got room at this table for a couple more guys?" Abraham said, squeezing himself in without waiting for an answer.

"Sure, sit down," Cara said, and everyone held their breath until Mike decided whom he was going to sit next to.

JEAN

THE SPRING SEMESTER of Brooke's sophomore year was looking infinitely better than the fall semester had been. She was taking two biology courses, a psychology course, and a class on Darwin. It was a lot of work, especially with the labs in biology, but she didn't appear to have anywhere near the demands of the fall semester and, so far, none of the unexpected problems.

There were days in the fall semester that, due to her schedule, Brooke would be in class from eight-fifteen in the morning until nine o'clock at night. Being in her chair for long periods of time like that wasn't good for the integrity of her skin. She had hundreds of pages of text to read each day and response papers to write every week. She was overworked, overwhelmed, and exhausted. I was getting concerned.

"You don't have to be a hero, Brooke. If this is getting to be too much, just say the word. We can take some time off if you need it."

"I'm okay, Mom," she'd tell me. "I can do this, I know I can do this."

The demand of the long days in class and the grind of the many hours of studying were further complicated by the fact that she was having difficulty breathing at night. Normally I was up with Brooke three or four times a night adjusting her position in bed or just taking care of other personal needs, but with her breathing problems, it had gotten to the point where I was up most of the night with her just trying to keep her airway clear. Neither one of us was getting much sleep.

It wasn't unusual for me to fall asleep in the lecture hall. I had learned to grab sleep where I could and when I could, but as the semester progressed, I began to notice that Brooke was falling asleep in class as well. That was something she never did. I thought it was the long days and lack of sleep but decided to have her tested just in case. When the results of the blood work came back, it showed that she had a pretty bad case of mononucleosis.

The doctor said that she had to rest, but I knew how difficult that was going to be for her. The amount of work Brooke had to do at Harvard was staggering, and with her, it always took much longer. I wasn't sure whether she should take a leave of absence and we should go home, or whether she should stay and try to rest at school. If we left, I knew how upset she would be, but if we stayed, I thought that maybe we wouldn't be doing the responsible thing.

"Your health is most important, Brooke, you can always make up a course."

"I'll be all right, I'm feeling better already. I'll get to bed earlier and I'll listen to my books on tape in bed and I'll do my papers on the weekends if I have to. I can rest here just as easily as I can rest at home."

"You won't have to do the work at home that you have to do here."

"What will I do, sit in bed and just watch TV? Time passes at the same speed no matter what we're doing, so I may as well be doing something worthwhile. I don't know how much time I have, Mom, none of us do. I want to stay, it will be all right."

We did stay and we made it through. Would I have done it again? Maybe. Would Brooke have? Absolutely. We were now already halfway into the spring semester and Brooke was feeling good. She felt strong, was enjoying her classes, and loved being with her friends.

BROOKE

"SOMEONE'S AT THE DOOR, BROOKE," my mother shouted to me from the kitchen while I was working on my computer. "Were you expecting someone?"

"Not that I know of," I said.

My mother answered the door and it was Cara and she was frantic. She was under a lot of pressure to finish her thesis and everything was going wrong.

"My computer is freaking out, and there are ants all over my room."

"Ants?" my mother said. "I haven't seen any ants."

"They're coming in through my window and are just in my room. Of course nobody else has them but me. I just needed to get out of that room and get to someplace sane," she said.

"You call this place sane?" I said. "Compared to what, the snake pit?"

"No, the ant farm," she said.

Cara stayed for a while until she calmed down. We asked her if she wanted to spend the night because of the ant problem. At first she hesitated because she didn't want to impose, but then, after thinking about it, she decided to take us up on our offer.

She went back to her room to get her pajamas and a change of clothes. We sat up for a couple of hours, just talking. Cara loved to talk and I liked that. I had been in my chair for a number of hours and sometimes when I sit in one position for a long period of time, I get muscle spasms. My legs start to move uncontrollably until I can either shift my position or someone can grab them to calm them down.

"Run, Forrest, run!" Cara shouted looking at my legs and imitating the little girl from the movie *Forrest Gump*. She had seen this happen to me before and I think she was just waiting for the opportunity to say that line. We all laughed and I was happy that Cara felt comfortable enough to say that to me. She was the first girl I had really gotten close to since my accident.

"Do you need to get Brooke back to bed?" Cara asked my mother, realizing that I was probably getting tired.

"Actually, she really should hit the sack," my mother said.

"Can I help you, Jean?" Cara asked.

"Who's Eugene?" my mother said, trying to be funny in her own silly way.

Cara gave her a look that told her in no uncertain terms that her joke was terrible.

"It's late," I said. "What did you expect?"

After my mother and I took care of a couple of personal things, Cara came into my room to help get me back to bed. She was curious to learn how my mother did it and wanted to help out. After I got settled, my mother went into her room and Cara pulled up a chair and we talked for a little longer.

"Do you ever fight with your mother?" Cara asked me.

"That depends on what you mean by 'fight,'" I said. "We're human and are subject to the same stresses and strains that everyone else is, probably more so because we're always together. She gets upset when I'm sad and I feel guilty when I know she's missing my father and my family, but fight, no, not really."

"Come on, I find that a little hard to believe. You're with each other twenty-four hours a day, and you don't fight?" she said.

"My mother and I are very different from each other in a lot of ways, and those differences can create problems. She's always hot and I'm always cold. She wants the window open and I want it shut. She's a morning person and I like to stay up at night. She won't shut up in the morning and I won't shut up at night. We both get PMS and become irritable with each other when we're under pressure, and we have our differences of opinion, if that's what you mean," I said.

"Spoken like a true Harvard student," Cara said. "That's just a euphemistic way of saying that you've had fights."

"No, not really, we couldn't do what we're doing if we fought. One of us would have packed it in a long time ago. I've got nothing to hide from you, Cara, you're my friend and I would tell you anything. There's nothing special about it, we're like every other mother and daughter except for maybe just one thing."

"What's that?" Cara asked.

"I've thought about this a lot and this might sound crazy to you, but I've never been afforded the luxury of being able to really fight with my mother."

"That is a little crazy. I don't get it," Cara said.

"Okay, let me put it this way. When do most girls fight with their mothers? It's when they're growing up. And what do they usually fight about? They fight about when they can start wearing makeup and how much they can put on. They fight over having boyfriends in the house, going on dates, and staying out past curfew. They squabble over getting that first job, a driver's license, and borrowing the car. They fight over the rites of passage that I never had. Most girls don't realize it, but those fights are luxuries."

"Is that it?" Cara asked.

"No, not quite. As much as I would have loved to have had those luxuries, sometimes it takes a situation like the one my mother and I are in to understand how unimportant all those luxuries really are. None of them are ever worth fighting over. After my accident, my mother and I almost lost each other. We know that anything can happen at any time. She's thankful that I'm still alive and I know how blessed I've been to have her in my life. We can bicker, we sometimes lose patience with each other, and we can get irritable for one reason or another, but we try not to waste our time on the small stuff. Unfortunately, what happened to me made both of us see more clearly and it doesn't have to be that way. What I'm trying to say is that it shouldn't have to take a horrible accident for any of us to see what's really important. We all have to try to learn something from the events that occur in our lives, and that's what I think we all need to understand."

"That's it?" Cara asked again.

"That's pretty much it," I said. "Except for the fact that both of us are too tired to fight. Who's got the energy for that?"

"You must be tired," Cara said. "I know I am. I think I'll get some sleep, too. It's going to feel weird sleeping alone tonight," Cara said.

"What?" I said, expecting to get some juicy piece of information that I didn't know before.

"I won't have my ants to cuddle up with tonight," she said, walking out of my room with an "I gotcha" grin on her face.

BROOKE AND I WAITED by the Garden Street entrance for Ed to arrive. It was a two-hour drive from the ferry in New London to Harvard Square. We could always figure, based on which ferry he was taking, what time he would pull up to Currier House. Today was no different. Ed pulled up within a couple of minutes of the time he said he would be there.

I always felt like a schoolgirl when I was waiting for Ed to come up to visit. I was forty-six years old and felt like I was sixteen. That was how old I was when we first met and I couldn't believe that thirty years later, I was still feeling the same way. Maybe it was the fact that we were separated from each other and we only got to see each other on the weekends; all I know is that when I saw the van pull up, my heart would start to pound, my hands would start to sweat, and I would have trouble restraining myself from jumping up and down. Invariably, though, it wouldn't go unnoticed by the girls in the house.

"Getting a visitor this weekend, Mrs. E," I would hear with a giggle after one of the girls would notice that my hair was a little darker than it had been the day before.

"George coming?" Cara would say, batting her eyelashes and puckering her lips after having noticed that I had just painted my nails.

Cara had started calling Ed "George" because Carl, the head of shuttle services, had forgotten Ed's name and called him George by mistake. Cara just thought it was hysterical and decided she would call him George from that point on. It may have been unwitting poetic justice on Carl's part, or it just may have been his subtle payback for having been called Cal by Ed when they first met.

I would even get a razzing from Diane and Honey.

"Hot date tonight?" or "I feel love in the air" would be standard remarks that I would get from them when I came into the dining hall wearing a dress instead of sweatpants and a sweatshirt.

Even though the girls had a lot of fun teasing me, they all knew that it was difficult for Ed and me to be apart. Even Chris the chef recognized the difficulties and planned a special meal for Ed and me. With the help of his wife and some of the ladies in the dining hall, Chris planned a romantic dinner for the two of us. A private table was set up in the dining hall with linens, flowers, and a bottle of wine. Chris prepared our favorite Italian meal, and from the appetizers and bread to the Italian pastries for dessert, it was wonderful. Even though Brooke was within earshot, it gave Ed and me some quiet time. We had time to hold hands, reminisce about the past, and recognize, despite the difficulties we had in our life, just how lucky we were.

BROOKE

EVERY SPRING, each house at Harvard has its own spring formal. It's like a high school prom, but all the students in the houses go, not just the seniors. Everybody dresses up in gowns and tuxedos and they go to a gala-like affair usually held at a hotel or catering hall in Boston. The spring formal is something the students look forward to and it usually marks the end of the school year. In my sophomore year, plans had begun early in the semester to secure a place for the Currier House spring formal. The place that was ultimately decided upon was the Bay Tower Room: a ballroom on the top floor of the Prudential Center, right in the heart of Boston. I had heard that the Bay Tower Room was similar to New York City's Windows on the World on the top of the World Trade Center because it had huge windows all around it that allowed you to see the entire city of Boston.

At the end of my sophomore year I was still very close to Jon, Neil, and Brent, but since my first semester in Currier, I had also grown close to both Abraham and Mike. I was seeing a lot of both of them; we ate dinner together, watched movies and talked. Our relationships, albeit platonic, meant a lot to me.

By April, everyone was talking about the spring formal and making plans for it. Cara and I would talk a lot about it at meals; she always wanted to know if I was going. I would always tell her that I didn't think I was. I felt that no one was going to ask me to go and I was reluctant to go without a date. As much as I really wanted to go and was being encouraged to go, I didn't think I would.

It was May 1, the last day of class in my sophomore year, and the formal was exactly one week away. It was about nine o'clock at night, Brent was over, and there was a knock at the door. It was Mike, who had just come back from playing basketball. While Brent was in the living room and my mother was in the kitchen, Mike asked if he could talk to me privately. We went into my room, he sat down on my bed, and he started to talk.

"So, Brooke, what do you think about the formal next week?" he asked me.

"What do you mean?" I asked, not sure what he was getting at. I never got the impression that formals were Mike's kind of thing, but there were always girls after him and I thought that maybe he was leaning toward going.

"Well, are you going?"

"I don't know, I don't think so," I said.

"Well, what would you think about going with me and being my date?" Mike asked.

I couldn't believe what I was hearing, and if he hadn't been such a good friend of mine, I would have thought it was a joke.

"Are you serious?" I asked, a little skeptical and a little embarrassed.

"Of course I'm serious. What do you say?"

At first I didn't know what to say and was a bit flustered. Mike and I had talked about a lot of different things, but this was the first time I didn't know what to say to him.

"I'm very touched, Mike, that's so nice of you, but I don't think I can do that," I said.

"What!" Mike said, I think a little surprised. "Why not?"

"There are a lot of reasons. You can go with any girl you want, why would you want to go with me? And this is going to be your last formal, you should go with someone you really want to go with. I don't know if you'll be able to have a good time with me," I said.

"What are you talking about?" Mike said. "I wouldn't have asked if I didn't want to go with you. In fact, I'm not going unless you go with me."

"I don't know, Mike, I—"

"I can't believe this!" Mike said, interrupting me. "I'm not taking no for an answer. That's it. We're going. Your job is to just pick out a restaurant that you want to go to before the formal. End of discussion."

Mike left, and I began to think about what had just happened. I was asked to go to the formal with one of the best-looking guys I had ever met, but something wasn't right. Not with him, with me. The more I thought about it, the more I understood the real significance of what had happened. The emphasis that I had put on the situation was misplaced. It didn't really matter what Mike looked like, it was what he had done that was important. The fact of the matter was he had accepted me for who I was and not for what I looked like, and that was the message I had been trying to teach people ever since my accident. It took a handsome Slovakian fencer to teach me a lesson I didn't think I needed to learn. He was, truly, another Michael in my life.

After Brent left, I called Cara to tell her what had happened and she was thrilled.

"Well, then, can I double-date with you guys?" she said.

"Sure," I said, "but you didn't tell me you had a date. Who is it?"

"Your mother," she said. "We're all going to have a great time. I can't wait to go shopping for shoes," she said, laughing.

JEAN

"REED'S HERE, and he's got two big bags of laundry," I shouted to Brooke, who was at her computer working on a paper for her Gen Ed 105 class. Brooke was into her junior year and Reed was a full-fledged freshman.

"How are your classes going, sweetheart?" I asked, starting to sort the colored clothes from the whites.

"They're fine, Mom, but don't do that, I didn't bring my clothes over for you to do them."

"You know that if you separated your clothes before you put them in the bags, you would make your life so much easier."

"Who's got time for that, Mom? It doesn't make any difference, I just throw everything in the machine together, anyway."

"So these boxers are supposed to be pink," I said, holding up a pair of underpants that looked as if they could only be worn on Valentine's Day.

"It doesn't matter, nobody sees me in them anyway," Reed said.

"You know that's just what a mother needs to hear, Reed," I said with a hint of relief after hearing that admission.

"Hey, Reed, how ya doin'?" Brooke said, wheeling over to see her brother. "I missed you," she said.

"I was here just last weekend and I talk to you almost every night," he said, bending over and kissing her on the cheek.

"I know, but that doesn't mean I still can't miss you," she said with a pout that told him that it was something that he couldn't tell her to stop doing.

Reed had decided to go to Tufts University, which was only five minutes away from where we were. He would try to visit once a week, and Brooke and I were so happy that he lived close by and we were able to see him so often. It almost seemed to make up for some of the time I thought we had lost.

"I'm taking this great class this semester, Reed," Brooke said, on her way into the living room to show him the paper she was working on. "It's called Gen Ed 105 and it's taught by Professor Coles, who I love, and I have this great TF, a guy named Duane, who's teaching the section for the class. We're reading works by Raymond Carver, John Cheever, Ralph Ellison, you remember Uncle Ralph," she said, pretending we were actually related, "and Flannery O'Connor. We then have to write papers applying what we've read to our own personal lives. I love it; it's almost a cathartic experience. It's funny, but I wasn't originally going to take that class but, you remember my friend Jon from Hawaii, he talked me into it. I'm in the same section with him, Neil, you met Neil the crew guy, and another guy named Chris, who Jon introduced me to last year. I think you'll meet Chris tonight at the a cappella concert. We have tickets for an eight o'clock show at Sanders Theater."

It was wonderful to see Brooke reunited with her brother and we loved having Reed up in Boston, but there was also a downside to it. Ed was still in New York and we were all up here. Ed and Reed had bonded during the two years they were together without us. They would eat together, and sometimes Reed would even get dinner started before Ed got home from work. I'm not really sure though, whether it was Reed's attempt to be helpful or just his best line of defense against Ed's cooking. Reed was good company for Ed and was just as much support for him as Ed was for Reed. Kysten was still living at home, but she was working two jobs and didn't get home until very late at night. She was also dating someone, and most of her time was spent with him. Ed and I spoke every night on the phone, usually for hours, and he came up on the weekends, but during the week he was home by himself. He never complained, but both Brooke and I knew that he was lonely and we were both very upset about that.

"Reed!" I shouted into the living room. "I know that no one sees you in your underwear, but whose bra is this mixed in with your laundry?"

"What!" Reed shouted, running in to see what I was talking about.

"Don't worry, I'm just kidding." I said, laughing at the panicked look on his face.

"COME ON, LET'S GO," my mother said, trying to get Reed and me off the computer. "The shuttle is here and we're going to miss the start of the show."

We were going to the a cappella concert at Sanders Theater and Joe was picking us up. Joe was one of the shuttle bus drivers my mother and I had grown so fond of. There was Carl, the head of shuttle services; Bob, who I liked to think of as my grandfather; Kevin, the retired cop who was always so helpful to us; Bab, his name was really Bob but with his Boston accent it always sounded like he was saying Bab; and of course Joe. Joe was Portuguese, but his heritage was only barely detectable. There was a hint of Portuguese in his accent, but living in Boston had taken care of most of that. He lived in the area with his young family who we loved to hear about and he loved to talk about. Joe was in his twenties and his passion was motorcycle riding. He was thin but wiry, and always liked to show off how well he was able to handle my chair.

"So where are we off to tonight, Brooks?" he said with his legs outstretched, emphasizing the fact that he was muscling my chair onto the lift.

"Sanders Theater, Joe. We're going to another a cappella concert. You've met my brother, Reed, haven't you, Joe?" I thought he had, but I just wanted to make sure.

"Oh, yeah, last week, how you doin', Reed," he said as he locked down the wheels of my chair to the floor of the van.

Joe always called me Brooks. It was something that must have gotten started when we first met him. My mother and I didn't realize he was calling me that until it was really too late to say anything. Neither one of us wanted to embarrass him or make him feel bad, so we just let it continue. It was also something that my friends caught on to very quickly, and soon everyone was calling me Brooks.

Joe dropped us off at the usual place between the Science Center and Memorial Hall. Sanders Theater was attached to Memorial Hall and was one of my favorite places to go to at Harvard. It was old, beautiful, and rich in history. We had heard concerts there, listened to guest speakers, and I even took some classes there. The theater is constructed entirely of wood and it almost has the feel of the Shakespeare's Globe Theatre, but it's more ornate than that. The railings on the balcony are intricately carved, and in addition to the omnipresent VE RI TAS Harvard insignia, there are Latin inscriptions carved above the stage. Two larger-than-life white statues of men in togas anchor each side of the stage. Since Reed was thinking of majoring in Latin and the classics, I asked him to translate the carvings:

"Toga . . . party . . . bring . . . your . . . own . . . beer," Reed said, emphasizing each word as if he were actually translating and before I realized he was only putting me on.

We got settled near the entrance in an area off to the right of the stage where my wheelchair fit comfortably and I wouldn't block anyone.

"Well, hello, Miss Ellison, how y'all doin'!" I heard a voice coming toward me with a deep rich southern accent. "That could only be one person I know," I said to Reed, turning my chair toward the entrance. It was my friend Chris, who had come in with his roommate, Mike. Chris and Mike were both a year behind me and I had only met them a few months before the end of my sophomore year. They both, however, had already made a lasting impression on me. Chris was from Florida, was very handsome, tall, and had light brown hair that was long enough to either slick back or brush down. Chris's big brown eyes were captivating and engaging and, when he spoke, he could enliven any conversation. Chris and I had a great deal in common. We shared similar beliefs, and we both felt in tune with the other's personal experiences. He was ambitious and had political aspirations, and his ambition always came with a smile and his heart was always in the right place.

Mike, who I had also met through Jon, was a few weeks older than I was but was in the class behind me. He was from Nebraska, but his midwestern accent was barely perceptible. He was tall and thin, having been a hurdler on the track team, had short, curly brown hair and a warm and friendly way about him. When I spoke to Mike, I knew he was listening. He was always so present, and when I was with him, he made me feel like I was the only other person on the planet. Mike and I became friends very quickly and we would get together often for heart-to-heart conversations.

I introduced Reed to both of them and I was happy that Reed was getting to know my friends. We talked a few moments before Chris and Mike went to take their seats.

"Don't forget we have to get together and talk," Mike said on his way to finding his seat. "I'll call you," he said. "Nice to meet you, Reed."

"Yeah, me too, Reed, nice to meet you. Let's all get together for a cup of coffee at Loker sometime soon," Chris said with a big smile, pumping Reed's arm with a hearty handshake.

"Nice to meet you, too, guys," Reed said. As Chris walked away, Reed turned to me and whispered, "He's the most enthusiastic guy I think I've ever met."

"I wouldn't be surprised if Chris is holding some office in Washington someday, Reed, and Mike, all I can say about him is that he's already become another Michael in my life."

WHENEVER ANYONE ASKS ME what it's like for Brooke to get through Harvard, I say to them: try to imagine being in a chair with your feet bound and your hands tied behind your back. Then imagine being on a machine that gives you thirteen breaths per minute and doesn't allow you to sigh or take a deep breath when you feel you need one. Then imagine never being able to use the bathroom or the shower when you want to, to brush your teeth, feed yourself, scratch an itch, or wipe your eyes if you need to cry. Imagine never having any privacy, not being able to be physically intimate, or never being able to hug someone when you really want to. Compound that with sleepless nights when you are unable to breathe, equipment failures that threaten your life, and wheelchair malfunctions that leave you stranded in bed. Then put yourself in one of the most rigorous academic settings in the world and ask yourself to read thousands of pages of text without being able to turn the pages; attend lectures, seminars, and labs in all kinds of godawful weather, study, prepare papers, take tests, and then do an original independent research thesis, submit it on time, and ultimately defend it. That will just start to scratch the surface of what it's like for Brooke to get through Harvard.

Brooke wanted to do her senior thesis on something she thought would be meaningful not only to her but to others who might benefit from her work. Near the end of her junior year she decided that she would do her thesis on a subject that she had some experience with, a concept that had been at the very core of her survival. She decided she would do her research on hope. She had always believed that hope had gotten her to where she was. She had always felt that without hope, the ability to resolve problems and overcome obstacles was significantly impaired. She wanted to study hope and come up with viable scientific data that would help corroborate what she already believed to be true: that hope fosters resiliency. She wanted to determine if hope was something that could be taught and learned so that kids who faced difficult challenges in their lives could have something they could rely on to help them through. She started doing her research before her junior year ended and planned to gather most of her data during the summer before her senior year. At about the same time that she started to develop her thesis, however, she started to develop a pressure sore at the base of her spine.

For anyone unfamiliar with pressure sores, they are spots on the skin where the tissue breaks down and a wound develops. They primarily occur in hospital patients who can't get out of bed and to people in wheelchairs who can't shift their position. For someone in a wheelchair it can be devastating. These sores can develop very quickly, virtually overnight to people who are paralyzed because they usually cannot feel them developing. Brooke had developed sores from having slept in the wrong position or sometimes for just having had a shoe on too tight. I had always been able to treat them myself and they would usually heal within a week or so. The sore that she developed near her coccyx bone just wouldn't go away.

It started in her junior year as a small opening in the skin and I began treating it right away. It was in such a bad spot, though, right where all her weight rested when she was sitting in her chair.

The problem was exacerbated by the fact that she had lost a lot of weight and didn't have all the extra cushioning that she once had there. The coccyx bone was pressing against her skin from the inside and her weight in the chair was creating pressure on the outside. I continued to treat the sore through the end of her junior year, but it didn't seem to be getting any better.

When we got home for the summer, Brooke got started on her thesis by studying any research that had already been done in the areas of hope and resiliency and by testing hundreds of high school students using scales designed to measure hopefulness, hopelessness, and resiliency. While she gathered the data and analyzed the results, I treated her sore. I battled it in the morning when she woke up and at night before she went to sleep. It was a battle I wasn't winning, so we had some doctors look at it. Brooke was seen by a regular surgeon, a plastic surgeon, an orthopedic surgeon, and a wound care specialist. The opinions varied in prognosis and in suggested courses of treatment. All had agreed, however, that it was much worse than I had thought. Pressure sores are like icebergs: What you see on the surface of the skin does not necessarily reflect what's going on underneath. Once the sore had been completely cleaned out, Brooke was left with an opening in her skin that was as round as a silver dollar and almost as deep.

A couple of the doctors wanted to do surgery as quickly as possible and even felt that a portion of her coccyx bone might have to be removed if an infection had reached the bone. Some had suggested IV antibiotics; others felt that a strong oral medication would be sufficient. There were differing opinions as to whether Brooke should return to Harvard for her senior year. They felt that if she had surgery, she would be in the hospital for six weeks; afterward, she would be in bed on her side for at least a couple of months. Brooke was upset, angry, and would have no part of it. We knew that we couldn't put Brooke in a medically dangerous situation, but for her to stop living her life the way she wanted to because of this additional obstacle would have been completely contrary to her character.

We decided to develop a game plan and got everyone involved. Anne Marie, Brooke's physical therapist, and Deneen, her occupational therapist, were wonderful, working diligently with us to try to solve the problem. She had pressure tests to develop a seating system that would relieve the pressure on that area. Anne Marie and Deneen both came to the doctors' offices with us to help develop a protocol that would be the least invasive. We all knew, and so did the doctors, that Brooke wanted to get back to school and finish what she had started. We chose a course of treatment that would require a lot of work and persistence from me in treating the wound, oral antibiotics, and regular treatments from a surgeon at Harvard. She wasn't going to have surgery and we made arrangements to go back to school.

BROOKE

WHENEVER ANYONE ASKS ME how I feel about my mother going to Harvard with me I say to them: Imagine working at something twenty-four hours a day, seven days a week, often without sleep. Then imagine taking care of yourself and then all of the personal needs of someone else—bathing them, feeding them, brushing their teeth, combing their hair, scratching an itch if they have one, and wiping their eyes and nose if they need it. Then imagine doing all that when you're sick and when you feel that you can't even lift yourself out of a chair. Imagine not having any privacy, not being able to take a break or walk away when you feel you need to, and not seeing your family and the man you love for long periods of time. Imagine dealing with the heart-aches of watching someone you love struggle and cope with the indignities of life. Then imagine doing it with a smile and with laughter and with a selfless love that is inspiring to watch. That might just start to scratch the surface of how I feel about my mother going to Harvard with me.

When we got back to Harvard, I knew my senior year was going to be a tough one. My mother was working very hard treating my pressure sore; she would work on it every morning and every night. She would pack it and treat it and make sure that I was off it as much as she could. When we first met Dana, a surgeon affiliated with Harvard Health Services, it was at her office to have my wound checked. She saw how difficult it was for us to get to her, so she offered to come to us. She came to our room on Fridays with her nurse, Jamie, to monitor my mother's work and to clean and further treat the wound. She was kind, understanding, and supportive, and she was a tremendous help.

I continued to work very hard on my thesis but I also had to stay out of my chair as much as I could. I would go to class, work on my computer, and then get back to bed as soon as I could. This not only made getting my work done more difficult but also cut down on my ability to socialize. My friends knew the problem that I was having and would come and sit in my bedroom and talk and hang out with me. Cara, who had graduated but was back up in Cambridge and working, would come over after doing a pastry run to Mike's Italian Pastry Shop in the North End of Boston. We would eat and talk and watch movies. My friends became used to seeing me in bed and they wouldn't think anything of it. They'd just come by, pull up a chair, and start telling me about their day.

There were times, though, when things would just get to me. All the work I had to do, my thesis, the sore and having to be in bed because of it, came to a head around Valentine's Day. Valentine's Day is a day I like to see come and go as quickly as possible. It's a great day for people who are in romantic relationships, but they are the ones who don't really need it. It's a terrible day for people who aren't romantically involved because it only emphasizes the fact that they're not.

Kysten, who had just broken up with her boyfriend, decided she wanted to come up with our cousin Kelly to visit us. Kelly, like the rest of my cousins, is very close to us. It was Cultural Rhythms Weekend, and that, along with the Arts First Festival weekend in May, is one of the two big weekends in the spring semester. Kysten and Kelly drove up, got lost of course, finally found us, and spent the weekend. Kysten and I had an opportunity to talk.

"Mom was saying that you've been a little sad lately and things are starting to get to you a little bit," she said.

"No more than usual."

"Did Valentine's Day have anything to do with it?" she asked.

"I guess so. I hate that day," I said.

"You and twenty million other people," she said. "Kelly and I were talking about it on the way up here, and I feel pretty much the same way she does. If it happens, great; if it doesn't, what are you going to do," she said, throwing her arms up in the air in resignation. "We have to make the most of what we've got and be happy with ourselves. After this last breakup, I'm just about convinced that I'll never be in a permanent relationship. You know what, though? I think I've got a lot to offer and I'm going to be all right even if I never have one. We're here for only a short time and we don't have a lot of time to waste wishing for things we don't have. You know what else, Brooke, if I think I've got a lot to offer, then just think about how I feel about you. I know that I don't say this often, but I'm so proud of you."

I felt that Kysten wasn't just talking, she really meant what she was telling me. I knew I had heard this before, but usually it was from my mother or father, who had been in a loving relationship, it seemed, since the beginning of time. Neither one of them was going through what Kysten and I were experiencing.

"I'm sorry that what happened to me happened," I said. "Not because of what it did to me but because of what it did to you and everyone else. I know how hard these ten years have been for you and the impact that it has had. I wasn't the only loser in this."

"Maybe we both came out as winners," she said. "We both had things to overcome and we did it. In the total scheme of things, not getting flowers on Valentine's Day doesn't mean a whole heck of a lot, does it? We've got each other, don't we?"

"Yes we do, and I love you," I said.

"I love you, too," she said.

When you really think about it, we're all in this big mess together, aren't we. It's not the kind of relationship we're in that matters, it's just the fact that we're in them that counts. We can touch each other's lives in so many different ways, and that's what we really need to remember. We need to be here for each other, help each other when we can, and love each other. That's all that's really important, nothing else really matters.

BROOKE HAD BEEN WORKING very hard on her thesis while I had been working very hard on her sore. It wasn't getting any worse, but it didn't seem to be getting that much better either. Brooke's thesis seemed to be making more progress than her sore was. The crunch to get her thesis in on time, however, was becoming all-consuming for Brooke. It was very demanding for her to do, and it was excruciating for me to watch. In early March, just a week or so before she was to submit her thesis, Ed called us. He told us that Brooke's friend Thomas, the boy she liked in Little League and her friend since elementary school, had been killed in a car accident. We were devastated. We put everything on hold and went home for the funeral.

"My thesis doesn't seem quite as important as it did a week ago," Brooke said to me on our way back up to Harvard.

"Nothing seems important when you're facing life and death," I said. "Nobody knows that better than you."

"Sometimes we forget, Mom. Sometimes we get caught up in our day-to-day activities and we lose sight of the bigger picture. I'm going to dedicate my thesis to Thomas, Mom. What do you think?"

"I think he would like that," I said.

When we got back to school, Brooke finished up her thesis and submitted it to her advisers two days early.

"Mrs. Krieger would have been proud of me, Mom," she said when she turned it in. "I made the deadline with room to spare."

There were just a couple of weeks between the time Brooke submitted her work and the day she had to defend it. Brooke had to be at William James Hall, Harvard's psychology building, at twelve-thirty in the afternoon. Her defense was going to be in an office on the eleventh floor with her three advisers: Professor Leichtman, who was a developmental psychologist and had just given birth to her second child; Professor Baxter, who was a statistician and a neuroscientist who specialized in the biology of learning and memory; and Professor Noam, who was a professor of childhood education and an expert in resiliency. Brooke had worked with all three of them during the preparation of her thesis and they had all been very helpful and supportive. She was still nervous, though, and knew that since they were all experts in their respective fields, she was going to be asked some very tough questions.

I set up the overhead projector and got her slides in place and she began her presentation:

"This study is an investigation into the psychological constructs and social influences that most profoundly affect an adolescent's level of psychological resilience. Specifically . . ."

I flipped transparencies while Brooke went on to explain them.

"To assess the mean differences between groups, t-tests and ANOVAs were run on the mean scores per group for each inventory. On average . . ."

She went on to analyze charts and graphs and statistical tests and finished her presentation in just over thirty minutes. Her professors took about the same amount of time to question her. She was doing well. I was a mess.

The last question posed to her dealt with what she thought were the implications of her study results. She took a couple of moments and then responded:

"This study indicates that hope can be taught and fostered throughout childhood by way of an adult/child relationship, specifically a parent/child relationship. As children learn the fundamentals of hope and resilience from significant adults in their lives, it becomes evident that instruction, nurturing, and dedication can alter the outcome of a child's life. By teaching children the strategies to employ the factors involved in hope and resiliency, it is arguable that hopeful thinking and resilient attitudes can be instilled in future generations. This may make these children better able to pursue their set goals and overcome adversity. With proper teaching at home and in school, it is feasible that hopefulness and resilience can be maintained throughout a lifetime, even after one has faced difficult circumstances."

After Brooke finished up, we were asked to wait in the hall while her advisers conferred on her grade.

"You did great, Brooke," I said.

"It was okay," she said. "How come they didn't ask you any questions?" she said, looking up at me with a smile. "You know something, it doesn't really matter what I got. It's over and I did it and I'm relieved, but in the total scheme of things, it's really only small potatoes."

"Brooke, you can come in now," Professor Leichtman said, leaning out into the hallway.

Brooke made her way back into the office and I followed right behind.

"Congratulations, Brooke, you've earned summa cum laude, highest honors."

I wanted to pump my fists, jump up and down, and shout it to the world. Brooke was very happy and appreciative and she thanked all of her advisers.

"Congratulations, honey, you did it. You got summa!" I said after we left the office. "Aren't you excited?"

"Of course I'm excited," she said, and paused for a moment

as if her mind was in another place. "You know, Mom, Thomas was with me in there. We did it, Thomas," she said, "we did it."

BROOKE

FLOWERS AND LIT CANDLES held down white linen cloths that were draped over the tables in the dining hall. It was early May and the semester was nearly over, the year had come and gone, and my days at Harvard were drawing to a close. It was the senior awards dinner at Currier House, a night set aside just for the seniors that the house masters presided over. It's a special dinner in the house where all the seniors get dressed up and gather together for one last meal and to honor each other.

The dining hall staff had done their usual beautiful job setting up. Diane and Honey worked that night as well as Maureen and her son, Steve, two of our other favorites from the dining hall staff. It's one of those bittersweet nights when you know you're going to laugh but are certain that you're going to cry.

My mother and I went down to the dining hall early. I wanted to savor every last moment that I could while I was still there. We got set up at a table and everyone began to arrive. The Grahams came in with Simon, the senior tutor, and his wife, Diane. Simon was an astronomer from England and I loved to listen to him speak. My friends Jeff, Adam, Ben, and Sean entered the room like Ben Hur's chariot horses, Jeff anchoring the inside and Sean pulling the rest of them along.

Everyone was more relaxed than they had been in recent weeks. Theses had been submitted and defended, and there were just a few papers and final exams that had to be finished up. Most everyone knew what they were going to be doing after graduation. For most it was some form of graduate school, law and medical school mostly. Some had landed jobs in their areas of study and others were going to be working for various investment houses. The economy was booming and all the big firms had been recruiting very heavily on campus.

Some of the house tutors had gathered together at a table. Eileen, an economist who had studied at MIT and Oxford, was sitting with Donella, an M.D./Ph.D. in neurobiology, Jenn, a recent Ph.D. recipient in psychology, and Ayanna, a Ph.D. candidate in English. They had all been so helpful to me while I was at Currier.

"Hello, everyone, can we join you?" my friend Alex said as he approached the table with my friends Shirley, Sonali, and John.

We had all shared so many dinners together at Currier House, so it was only appropriate that we share this one as well. Alex is a spiritual soul who had taken a prior year off to do missionary work in Central America. We had spent many evenings discussing faith and the impact that it had on our lives. Shirley, whose parents were from Puerto Rico, was always a joy to have at the table. She was happy and loving and she always made me smile when I saw her. Sonali was a beautiful young woman of Indian descent. She had been so supportive of me when I was doing my thesis and, after I turned it in, we celebrated together with a sushi party. John, who is Korean and whose father is a minister, is so gentle and caring. He had always shown concern for both my mother and me and would go out of his way to help us whenever we needed it.

We all ate and talked. We reminisced about the years we spent at Harvard and in Currier House. While I was silently bestowing my own awards on the people in the room, the Grahams got up to present their awards. For each award recipient, they read a brief description of what the person had done and an explanation of why the person was deserving. It was read before the person's name was announced. We all had fun trying to guess who the person was before they could announce the name. We nailed it just about every time. The last award that was given for the evening was presented by Barbara Graham. She stepped to the podium and adjusted the microphone;

"For four years you have been in faithful attendance at Harvard classes and rendered steady service in support of learning and scholarship. . . ."

That could be anyone, I thought.

"You have graciously accommodated to life among the undergraduates of Currier House and Harvard College, and . . ."

Again, that could be anyone, I said to myself.

"Over these years you have been bound night and day to the sleepless schedule, endless exams and laboratories, countless papers and rounds of popular music. . . ."

It was when she said "popular music" that lights started to go on in the heads of everyone sitting at the table.

"You have given such service transparently and unobtrusively with immense good cheer and unselfish love."

I got a wink from Alex and a smile from Shirley.

"The masters, senior tutor, and tutorial staff of Currier House, Harvard University, proudly has awarded . . ."

There was a pause but everyone in the room already knew who it was.

"Jean Ellison the degree of Auditing Bachelor in Virtual Studies."

My mother was overwhelmed and could barely get up from the table to receive her award. Everyone in the room was standing and cheering. Barbara met my mother halfway to give her the award and they were both crying as they hugged each other. I couldn't stand or clap but the pounding of my heart made enough noise for everyone to know how I felt. The award that my mother got was not an official degree, it carried no academic weight, but that didn't matter. It represented the hard work she had done, the love she had given, and the respect she had earned.

My mother had always said that she wanted to teach and have an impact on kids other than her own. It was clear to me, and to everyone else in the room that night, that she had most certainly done that.

JEAN

ED GOT A CALL at one o'clock in the morning from his sister, Amy, who lived in Manhattan.

"I got the early edition of *The New York Times*," she said, "and Brooke and Jean are on the front page."

We knew the *Times* was going to run an article on us, we just didn't know where in the paper it was going to be.

A couple of weeks earlier, Brooke had gotten a call from the Harvard disability office saying that a reporter from *The New York Times* had contacted them looking for upcoming graduates with unique situations for a story he was doing. They had given him Brooke's name as a possibility and told him to contact her. As expected, the next day, after we had gotten back from class, he called. He spoke to Brooke for almost two hours on the phone and wanted to know as much as he could about her: her history, her life growing up on Long Island, her reason for choosing Harvard, and her experiences there. When she told him that she had attended Harvard with me and that she had been selected to give

one of the speeches at Senior Class Day, he became very interested. What was originally expected to be only a telephone interview became much more. The next day he made arrangements
to come up to Harvard to spend the day with us and he brought
along a photographer to take pictures.

"What does it say, what does it look like?" Ed said to his sister,
a little groggy from having fallen asleep on the couch.

"There's a great color picture below the fold of Brooke and
Jean," Amy said. "Jean's wearing a yellow sweater that matches
the yellow suit that Hillary Clinton is wearing in her picture with
Bill at the top of the page."

"Brooke and Jean are below the fold and the president's above
the fold," Ed said. "I'm going to have to talk to the *Times* about
that. What does it say?"

"The picture is below a headline that reads: 'An Unrelenting
Drive, and a Harvard Degree.' Let me read it to you," she said,
anxious to give him the details.

Amy read him the article and Ed immediately called me on
the phone. It was late, but I was up with Brooke anyway. He told
us as much as he could about it, but I didn't have a paper that I
could read. I called shuttle services, which still had guys on duty.

"Hello, shuttle services, Bab speaking."

"Hi, Bab," I said. I called him Bab instead of Bob without
thinking. "If you pass a newsstand in your travels, do you think
you could pick up a *New York Times* for me?" I told him why I
wanted it, and at about three in the morning, he knocked at the
door with his arms full of newspapers.

Brooke and I had been in newspapers before and we had gotten feedback from people when they read the articles, but no one
could have prepared us for what happened after that *Times* article
appeared. Brooke began receiving, literally from all over the

world, e-mails and phone calls from radio shows, newspapers, magazines, and television news shows all wanting to interview her and get her story. The article had mentioned that she was going to be giving a speech on Class Day and the media wanted to be there. It was overwhelming and certainly more than either one of us could handle. Rebecca, Sally, and Andrea from the Harvard news office were lifesavers. They got involved and started screening all the phone calls that were coming in. They also handled and coordinated all the media that wanted to attend the Class Day speech.

"This is one heck of a way to end a college career," I said to Brooke

"I don't understand what the big deal is, Mom," Brooke said. "I'm just a kid graduating from college."

The phone rang and I picked it up, ready to give the caller the phone number of the Harvard news office.

"Mrs. Ellison," I heard a man's voice on the other end.

"Yes, who's calling?" I said.

"It's David," he said.

"David? David who?" I asked.

"David from high school, can I please speak to Brooke?"

BROOKE

IT WAS STILL RAINING the morning of class day, after a torrential downpour the day before. Class Day is always the day before the official Harvard Commencement, but unlike commencement, Class Day doesn't require a ticket to attend, it's open to everyone. My father and Reed had come up earlier, but most of my family and friends from New York had battled the rain the night before. Kysten had driven up with my grandmother and my aunt Amy. Debby, John, and Zachary also braved the rain, as did my mother's friends Chris and Astrid from her teaching days. Deneen and Anne Marie, my therapist friends, and my aunt Margaret and uncle Lee were on their way up on the ferry and hoped to make it before the ceremonies started at two o'clock.

"Do you think I'm going to be able to speak in this rain, Dad?" I said to my father when he came into my room to talk.

"There's going to be an awful lot of disappointed media people if you don't," he said.

"Do you believe all this attention?" I said. "I don't understand it. We're even getting a police escort down to the Yard today."

"I know, your mother filled me in on that. It's for your protection."

"Yeah, it's really been crazy around here," I said. "And speaking of crazy things, did I tell you that David called me last week?"

"David . . . from high school?"

"Yeah, he said he read the article in the *Times* and wanted to congratulate me."

"What did you say to him?"

"I thanked him."

"That's it?"

"No, he apologized. After all these years, he apologized for what he did. He said he learned a lot in college and had wanted to call sooner, but he felt too awkward."

"What did you say?"

"I told him I forgave him, and that actually I had forgiven him a long time ago."

"It sounds like he may have learned something important in college, something you don't usually find in a textbook," my father said.

"I think we both did, Dad. Most of the important things we learn in life aren't found in textbooks."

The van had arrived with a police car and they brought the sun with them. The sky was clear and a deep bright blue, almost like a canvas that had been painted. It was almost too blue to be real.

My mother, father, Reed, and I went out to the van; everyone else had gone down to the Yard to get seats. Carl was standing near the van in his "uniform," a sports jacket, tie, khaki pants, and a pair of tasseled loafers. My mother and I watched and waited to see if Carl and my father would get each other's name right.

"Hi, Carl, nice to see you again," my father said.

"Hi, Ed, nice to see you, too."

That was a good sign, I thought.

"Your ride, my dear," Carl said, bowing and sweeping his arm toward the van.

Having Carl as our driver to the Class Day ceremony seemed perfect, since he had been the first person we met over four years earlier. Carl got me into the shuttle, he and my father locked me down, and we followed the police car down to the Yard. We made our way down Garden Street, and as we got closer to Harvard Square, the traffic started to build. The police escort turned on his siren and cleared the way for the van to get through.

"This is so embarrassing," I said to everyone in the van.

"Just enjoy it," Carl said. "It's not every day that you get something like this."

"Think of the sirens that you've had escort you in the past, Brooke," my father said. "Look how far you've come since then."

Carl drove the shuttle into the Yard through a private fire gate across from the Cambridge fire department and parked the van right in front of Thayer Hall. The police officer escorted us around the side of Memorial Church and up onto the stage where I would be giving my speech. I positioned myself next to the chairs where the class marshals and other speakers would be sitting. I was right next to my friend Justin, the senior class marshal, who was emceeing the event. We had about twenty minutes before the ceremony was scheduled to begin. From the stage, I looked out to an ocean of people stretching from the steps of Memorial Church, where I was, to the steps of Widener Library at the end of the Yard. There were over twenty thousand people, spread out across Tercentenary Theater. There was an area to the right of the stage that was cordoned off. It was filled with cameramen, photographers, and reporters, snapping pictures and talking into microphones. Reed had gone down to sit with my sister and grandmother in his reserved seat in the second row. My mother had a seat behind me on the stage and my father stayed with me a few minutes before going down to his seat.

"I don't know what everyone is expecting, Dad," I said, looking out at the mass of people and reporters.

"What do you mean?" my father said.

"With my speech," I said. "I'm afraid that with all this attention and expectation, everyone's going to be disappointed. It's not a great oration, it's just something I want to say from my heart."

"You can't go wrong with anything that comes from your heart, Brookie-Love. It's going to be fine. I love you."

My father kissed me on my forehead and went down to take his seat. I was nervous and tried to go over my speech in my head. I had memorized it, and I wasn't going to be using any notes. I was having difficulty concentrating and the audience was just a blur. My friend Joe, who was getting an award for his selfless

work with refugee kids, walked passed the stage. I remembered
the help he had given my mother and me during freshman week
when my wheelchair had broken down, and I began to pick out
faces in the crowd. I saw Jon and his family smiling at me. I saw
Neil, who had come up on stage to give me a kiss. I saw my
friends from Currier House. I saw my aunts Margaret and Amy
and I saw Debby and her family. Chris and Astrid, Deneen and
Anne Marie were smiling and looking up at me. I knew I was
with people I loved and who loved me. I began to feel better.

Justin approached the podium and addressed the audience.
He was wonderful and handled the crowd beautifully. He introduced speakers and other class marshals and time didn't seem to
exist. It was as if we were all just there, suspended in the moment.
Then I heard: "Please give a warm welcome to Brooke, who will
be giving her speech, entitled 'A Shared Confidence.' "

I felt my mother come up behind me to help me to the front
of the stage. I looked out into the crowd, closed my eyes for a
second, swallowed hard, and began to speak:

> When I arrived at Harvard four years ago, I arrived with my
> parents, like most other freshmen. Unlike everyone else, though,
> my father left but my mother didn't. The name tag on the door
> at 212 Thayer Hall said "Brooke and Jean Ellison." The initial
> reaction to this situation was usually one of confusion or some
> degree of disbelief. I think the idea of going away to college with
> your mother is a concept not readily embraced by most college
> freshmen. A mother's presence, albeit nurturing, can create a
> whole host of social problems for those seeking more than just
> academic enrichment. But my mother has been with me every
> hour of every day and has attended all of my classes from fresh-

man expos to senior thesis. I am a matriculated student; my mother is not. I will get a diploma, my mother will not. Has she been any less enriched than I have because of those two facts? Absolutely not.

When we first arrived here from New York, neither one of us knew what to expect. I was seventeen and my mother was forty-four and it was the first time away at college for both of us. We were frightened. We wondered whether we would fit into the Harvard community. Somehow, crisscrossing Harvard Yard in my wheelchair with my mother running behind me with my books and other paraphernalia didn't quite create an image of our blending into the Harvard landscape. There were times when I thought for sure that the statue of John Harvard was looking right at us and saying, "What in Heaven's name are you doing here?"

But as time passed, we came to understand that John Harvard was from a different time. We began to realize that our conspicuousness was not such a bad thing. Through the personal relationships that we formed we learned that some people's differences were just more subtle than others. We were a very visible affirmation that Harvard was a diversified community where all people were accepted no matter what they looked like, what they believed in, or whom they chose to go to bed with. The striking irony about this observation was that through the recognition of our differences came the realization that we were all the same. The basic need and desire to love and be loved exists in all of us. The beauty of the Harvard experience lies in the relationships that we have formed here.

We are all about to receive our diplomas, which represent many years of hard work. However, I dare say that once that *diploma has been matted, framed, and put on the wall the memories that it will evoke will not be of what it took to get it. You will think about the Yard and the Quad. You'll remi- nisce about Harvard Square and the houses in which you lived. You'll think of the Science Center, Sanders Theater, and ahhh, coffee at Loker; but most importantly, you'll think of the peo- ple—the people with whom you shared these places. The mem- ories that I have, my mother has. The relationships that I've made, my mother has made. From the professors and students to the bus drivers and dining hall staff, our lives have been enriched by all the people we have met.*

I would not be here if it were not for my mother and she would not be here if it were not for me. And so it goes. As much as we would like to take credit for our own accomplishments, none of us would be here had it not been for the efforts and caring of those who have helped us along the way. Our mutual dependence is so often misdiagnosed as self-reliance. Whether it was a parent or sibling, a friend or teacher or just someone who was able to say the right thing at the right time, none of us has escaped the love and caring of others. Both my mother and I have learned so much from all of you. What we hope you can learn from us and from each other is to take no one in your life for granted and delight in the moments that you spend together. Time is so brief and so precious and not one of us knows how life will unfold.

Ten years ago, when I was eleven years old, I was hit by a car. I was initially thought to be brain dead and no one expected me to live. I have been paralyzed from the neck down and on a respirator since that time. Tomorrow I will graduate from Harvard with my mother and all of you beautiful people. Mir- acles happen. They have happened to me and they are happening

to you. You need only look at the people in your lives in order
to see them.

  Congratulations, everyone, and God bless.

My mother came up beside me and she was crying. She helped me ease my chair back into place. I saw Justin next to me and he was standing and applauding and I realized that everyone was on their feet. At first I was embarrassed and didn't know what to think, but I looked down into the second row and saw my grandmother and thought about how she had cared for my sister and brother and how she had nursed my grandfather when he was so ill. I saw Kysten and Reed and thought about all they had been through and the sacrifices they had made. I saw my father standing and smiling with tears running down his cheeks and I thought about everything he had done to make this all work. I then looked up at my mother and I thought about her and me and how our relationship had grown and changed. She was my mother and I was her daughter, but she had become my closest companion and my dearest friend. I thought about all the joys and the sorrows we had been through together and I realized that the two of us were really just one. The world seemed so clear to me now; just as my mother and I were one, so too were we all. The bond that developed between us was really no different than those that bind us all. None of us is alone. We are not random dots of dust floating aimlessly without any greater purpose; we are all here for each other. I realized, as I looked out at the crowd and then at my mother, that I had an answer for her question, an answer that she really always knew. Our purpose here is to be miracles for each other.